THE PERFORMING ARTS
An Audience's Perspective

David P. Hirvela

Iowa State University

KENDALL/HUNT PUBLISHING COMPANY
4050 Westmark Drive   Dubuque, Iowa 52002

Contents

Preface

You are the most crucial element in the performing arts experience. You gather as audiences. The audience stimulates actors, musicians, dancers, directors, and designers to create and perform. Without your responses the performing arts do not exist. The audience is supreme. You are the crucial link that creates the performing arts.

How can you develop into knowledgeable, perceptive, and responsive audiences? Audience education is the answer. However, busily creative performing artists often ignore the learning needs of their patrons. Professional educators often overlook audience education in their zealous commitment to training young performers. This book will provide the information that will help your appreciation and understanding of a performing art. The book's focus is on *experiencing* the art rather than *doing* the art.

This book gives you the basic information that enables any general audience member to enjoy a specific performing art: theatre, music, dance, television, film, radio, and the recording arts. Some "good audience member" skills apply to all the performance arts. They are ways of perceiving, experiencing, and responding to performances. Audience psychology and sociology; the processing of verbal, visual, and auditory stimuli; listening; and specific methods to enhance responses to the performing arts will be discussed and illustrated. Other skills relate to the specific ways that each performing art asks us to perceive experience; understanding the unique qualities of each art will increase our knowledge of the arts. More detailed information about the performing arts will be found in the bibliography.

Throughout the book I will urge you to attend the performing arts. Nothing matches attending a performance. As the information from this book expands your knowledge and attendance enriches your experience, your overall appreciation for the performing arts should increase.

Your ability to evaluate performances will grow. Any arts experience evokes a response. You have no choice. This response functions as criticism. The best criticism is informed. Knowledge of the performing arts and of the perception process provides crucial information about them. Experiencing the various arts expands upon book knowledge. Knowledge plus experience leads to appreciation. From appreciation will arise an informed evaluative response. You should by the end of this book develop your responses to the performing arts far beyond the simple "I like it."

This book is aimed at people interested in gaining more insight into their performing arts' experiences and more understanding about methods of enhancing those experiences. Any introductory class in the performing arts would find this information a valuable supplement.

Acknowledgements

I want to thank all the people who contributed to the preparation of this book. Special appreciation goes to my friends and colleagues at Iowa State University who took time to review my manuscript, sharpen my writing, and improve my understanding: Jane Cox, Richard Kraemer, Phyllis Lepke, Mark A. Redmond, and Donald Simonson. To all the guest lecturers in THEATRE 106 (Introduction to the Performing Arts) who have contributed to my understanding and appreciation of the performing arts I express my gratitude; without you this book would not have been possible: Janice Baker, Clement Chow, Jane Cox, George Dowker, Patrick Gouran, Gregg Henry, Evelyn Jensen, Richard Kraemer, Phyllis Lepke, Geraldine Maschio, Wayne Mikos, Charles Oates, Laurie Sanda, David Stuart, Fritz Szabo, and Betty Toman. I have team-taught THEATRE 106 with Geraldine Maschio, Charles Oates, and Jane Cox; they have been stimulating companions in my study of the performing arts.

I also want to thank Iowa State University for the Faculty Improvement Leave, which supported the completion of the manuscript; Deb Tjelta for her clerical support; and Claudia Hale for administrative and emotional support throughout the writing process.

Finally, thank you to Allan John Deptula, whose faith in and support of my efforts enlivened my spirits throughout the entire writing process.

Introduction: Art and the Performing Arts

Art Experiences

The light reflected from the film screen illuminates dimly the two hundred people surrounding you. As the young woman dying from cancer says goodbye to her children on the screen, you are aware of your heightened emotional response: shortened breaths, tears, a muscular tension. A sense of sorrow and melancholy invades your whole being. As she feels, so do you. As this happens to you, you are only slightly aware of the two hundred people sitting around you. Yet you sense their similar feelings. The film ends. This sorrowful experience is over. Yet your mind remembers that experience. Over the next few hours or even days your mind will give meaning to the experience for your life. However, that sorrowful farewell will not be relived again, unless you see the movie again.

You are completely unaware of the stillness and your own solitude as you turn the page of the novel. Immersed in the struggles of the main characters, you are actively participating in their lives. You can see them. You experience their feelings. Descriptions of environments spring off the page. You are transported from your comfortable reading chair to places that you have never visited. Yet those places are easily visualized. And, if any section puzzles or if a "favorite part" especially pleases, you can go back again and again and reread it. If an idea or an image stimulates thoughts, your reading stops; you can reflect, returning to the page whenever you wish. The world of the novel becomes your world, fully realized by your imagination and available anytime you pick up that special book.

The round curves of the abstract stone sculpture grab your attention as you approach it. What does it mean? You do not know, but the object captivates your senses. The sculpture demands to be touched. Your hands caress its curves. The cool polished smoothness of the stone satisfies your touch. As you walk around it, you are aware that it looks different from

1

"The Left-Sided Angel" by Stephen De Staebler outside of the Parks Library at Iowa State University stimulates reactions as sculpture, one of the visual arts. (Photograph by Mike Doolen.)

the side and the rear. You step back several feet; its proportion and mass are different. Its serenity, its spherical completeness give you a sense of calm. You approach it again. One final touch. That tactile moment must be relived. You leave, knowing that someday you will return to this particular sculpture again.

The preceding descriptions capture three varying kinds of arts and the special conditions and behaviors that are part of experiencing them. Each encourages us to respond in special ways. The specific ways are determined by its nature, as ''art'' and as a ''form of art.''

What Is Art?

This question is complex. Artists, philosophers, and critics have argued about it from the beginnings of Western civilization. As audience members we need to understand art only as it has impact on our eventual appreciation of a performance. The following definitions of art distinguish that experience we call art, differentiate the various art forms, and contrast them from popular entertainment.

Functional Definition: The Forms of Art

Webster's New World Dictionary, © 1944, defines the differences among the various arts: art is the ''making or doing of things that display form, beauty, or unusual perception.'' Individual artists express form, beauty, and unusual perception by *doing* or *making* things. This simple differentiation separates the visual and literary arts from the performing arts.

The visual and literary artists *make* their art. It is fixed-in-time; the viewer or reader may revisit it at any time. What are these arts specifically?

The Visual Arts

*Painting   *Ceramics
*Sculpture   *Photography
*Graphic Arts   *Architecture

The Literary Arts

*Fiction: novel, short story
*Nonfiction: essay, biography, history, criticism
*Poetry
*Drama

In contrast the performing artists do their art. It exists in time, usually coinciding with the actual moment of performance. The audience members also experience the art only once—as it happens to them at the moment of performance. In most cases performances cannot be immediately reexperienced. What are these performing arts?

The Performing Arts

*Theatre
*Music
*Dance
*Mass Media
     —Film
     —Television
     —Radio

Twentieth century technology has developed another category for the performing arts: the recording arts. The performing arts may be recorded on video or audio tape. What once could only be received in a theatre or concert hall may now be experienced in our living rooms. In this way the recording arts are similar to the fixed-in-time literary and visual arts.

Artist's Definition: A Personal Perspective

Understanding art from the individual artist's viewpoint, i.e., what the artist is striving to express in one of the various art forms, gives the audience insights, which will enhance our experience of art. Writer, Sylvia Angus, defines art emphasizing the contribution of the individual artist:

> Art is the controlled structuring of a medium or a material to communicate as vividly and movingly as possible the artist's personal vision of experience.
>
> This definition, be it noted, allows for weak art or for great art, depending on the skill or stature of the artist. It does not allow any place for the random or totally unstructured. The key words are "controlled structuring." Experience, emotion, communication are all ingredients, but all are insufficient without the controlling mind which, alone, is capable of producing art.
>
> If there is no focusing, organizing intelligence behind it, there is no art in any meaningful sense of the word.

Angus' definition deepens our understanding of art, making us aware of the artist's centrality. Art is communication. It begins with the artist, who expresses a personal vision through the controlled structuring of a medium or material; it ends with the audience, who receives the artist's message. The audience completes the communication initiated by the artist.

Philosophical Definition: Art As a Form of Knowledge

Besides being an artist's "personal vision of experience" and a "making or doing of things exhibiting form, beauty, and unusual perception," art is also a form of knowledge. Art provides perceptions and insights about ourselves and the world. It serves as a way to understand the world. Art is similar to science in this way; only the methods of understanding are different. With art we gain understanding by participating aesthetically and empathically with the art form.

According to *Webster's New World Dictionary,* © 1974 aesthetics is a branch of philosophy dealing with art, its creative sources, its forms, and its effects. We gain knowledge from art by participating aesthetically with it. For example, experiencing theatre or music or dance lifts us from the hum-drum of our daily existence, exhilarates us sensually, and transports us to realms of emotion and thought. Art may confront us with the universal issues of our existence, those issues that cut across all human experience—love, death, family, sorrow, life's meaning. We may achieve these insights by participating with the performers and their arts. Aesthetic participation demands some knowledge of the art, an understanding of how to increase your aesthetic participation, and a willingness to allow your imagination to be stimulated through the senses. Aesthetic participation results in pleasure for the audience.

Empathy is the ability to share another's emotions or feelings, or the projection of your personality into the personality of another person or into an object in order to understand them better; with empathy you attribute to the other person or object your own emotions and responses. (*Webster's New World Dictionary,* © 1974, p.458) We also receive meaning from art by responding empathically with it. In theatre, film, and television as we empathize with the characters in a drama, we gain knowledge of human behavior and of the universal themes of human existence.

Aesthetic and empathic participation in art forms give us knowledge as surely as scientific enquiry does. What art has to say is serious and important. However, the arts do not present information with the accuracy of the scientific method. The arts are indirectly communicated to audiences, i.e., they present experiences but often do not fully explain them. 2 + 2 = 4 is a direct and easily understood message. The opening of Beethoven's *Fifth Symphony* is indirect and not fully understandable. However, art's meaning is accessible, if you understand its indirectness and accept the complexities and varieties of artistic interpretations.

Summary: The Purposes of Art

From the definitions several specific purposes for art are apparent. From the creator's viewpoint art communicates both thoughts and emotions. Whether the artist uses the "language" of dance, music, words, or images, art serves as the means to share ideas and feelings. The concept of "sharing" is crucial not only to the artist but also the art. Art does not exist without the audience, who completes the artist's act of communication.

For the audience art has the purpose of helping us better understand life in all its complexities. The universal concerns of human beings—life, death, love, conflict, relationships, and suffering—are the subjects of all art. By experiencing art the audience confronts these often ignored "great issues" and uses the experience to clarify them in their own minds.

Finally, art has the purpose of giving aesthetic and empathic pleasure to both the artist and the audience. Even if art did not stimulate the audience to think about life's great issues, art could exist on its own: "art for art's sake." The existence of art in its many forms provides much artistic and emotional pleasure for us.

By understanding the purposes of art we can integrate them into our experiencing of the arts as audiences. Knowing that art exists for a variety of reasons can expand our appreciation of novels, paintings, and the performing arts. These art experiences may produce a profound impact on our lives.

Art vs. Popular Entertainment

Art, by definition, is serious, i.e., it has something important to say. The artist communicates his thoughts and emotions so that the audience participates aesthetically and empathically and gains insights about the meaning of life. However, not every novel, painting, film, or song is art. All the art forms can function as popular entertainment.

What Is Popular Entertainment?

Popular entertainment is simply an amusement or a diversion for a mass audience, which uses currently dominant attitudes and interests, and integrates them with stereotyped characters, stock situations, and universally acceptable ideas. If successful, popular entertainment amuses the mass audience, but seldom offers new insights into life or raises any questions that might disturb the present attitudes of the audience.

Popular entertainment is easily identified. Think of most television dramatic or comedy series. Think of the vast number of films produced in the United States. Think of the music industry's ability to produce new songs, artists, and groups. All of these performing arts appeal to millions by giving people exactly what they want to see and hear.

Popular entertainment's subjects reflect the attitudes and interests of the present moment. The dominant interests—whether they be action adventure, violence, comedy, the family, romance, horror, or sex—change quickly like all fads. Although the content of popular entertainment changes, its structure has remained constant through time.

Popular entertainment's structure employs stereotyped characters, stock situations, and universally acceptable ideas. A stereotype embodies an over simplified or conventional pattern of behavior considered typical for a group, e.g. "absent-minded professors" or

6

"dumb jocks." In film and TV as examples of popular entertainment, this stereotyping of characters occurs often. Parents get portrayed as extremes: either the stupid, insensitive adult or the caring, perceptive dad or mom. Usually in film or TV, teenagers and children are bright, intelligent, and very funny.

Stock situations abound in drama/comedy that is popular entertainment. The number of films and television programs that show the "underdog" fighting insurmountable forces and winning is staggering. These films or programs always end happily with a clear, unambiguous victory for the "good guys" and punishment of the "bad."

Universally acceptable, non-controversial ideas abound in popular entertainment. Song lyrics are endless repetitions of the socially accepted views on love and romance: the abandoned can't stop loving their departed lovers; if you're "in love," you're nothing without your love; being in love is all the worth of life. Dialogue and ideas in TV drama reinforce the present attitudes toward love and life: the swinging single lifestyle of TV's "Three's Company" gave over to the family values of "The Cosby Show." "Rambo" defines for many people the correct foreign policy of the United States.

Popular entertainment amuses and entertains the mass audience by utilizing the elements of content and structure with energy and technical expertise; the entertainment product has the veneer of slick professionalism. Audiences immediately relate to and understand popular entertainment products. They reinforce audience's present beliefs and attitudes. However, popular entertainment offers no important new perceptions about life or art, and certainly will not raise any disturbing questions that challenges the audience's views.

Purpose of Popular Entertainment

The performing arts as popular entertainment helps us escape the problems and pressures of everyday existence. As many people who attend theatre or films say: "I go to the theatre to be entertained, not to deal with the problems of other people. I have enough problems of my own. I don't want to think when I go to the theatre. I just want to relax and have a good time."

Popular entertainment provides important moments of diversion in our lives. We can recall pleasant, happy moments with theatre, film, TV, music, or dance in the form of popular entertainment. Popular entertainment can be grouped with other recreational pastimes which allow us to escape the workaday world. However, if the performing arts are merely recreational and do not offer any additional appeals, they may be (and often are) dismissed as lacking any true significance.

All of the performing arts function as both art and popular entertainment. Knowledge about how the performing arts function as art or popular entertainment give us realistic expectations about performances. For example, knowledgeable and experienced audience members will not expect a piano recital or symphony orchestra concert to function like a rock concert, or a performance of *Romeo and Juliet* to produce the same results as a *Star*

Theatre, one of the performing arts, is experienced by an audience at the Guthrie Theater in Minneapolis, MN. (Courtesy of the Guthrie Theater, Minneapolis, MN.)

Wars movie. Knowledge and experience of the performing arts increases our enjoyment of any performance whether it is art or popular entertainment.

Contrasts: Performing vs. Literary/Visual Arts

What are the major differences between the performing arts and the visual/literary arts? One basic difference relates to how the art is experienced in time. The performing arts are *ephemeral* and *temporal;* the visual/literary arts are *fixed-in-time.*

When you watch a play in a theatre, the experience is happening in a defined period of time—"two hours traffic upon the stage" as Shakespeare said. After two hours the art of the production no longer exists, except in your memory. You may not re-experience that evening in the theatre. If you returned the next evening, the experience would be different: the actors would do different things; the audience would respond in different ways; the performance, which is theatre art, would be different.

Contrast the short-lived, temporary theatre event with the drama—the literary form—which was performed. The drama is unchanging; the playwright's words as written on the page are permanently fixed-in-time. You may return at your leisure to read them. They are changeless. The visual/literary arts allow us to return to experience them as often as we wish. The Mona Lisa's enigmatic smile will be the same each time we contemplate it.

The performing artist creates at the moment the audience experiences. The performance of a Mozart piano concerto in the concert hall happens to you immediately as the pianist and orchestra play. The visual/literary arts are considerably different. The novel or sculpture has been created long before you read or view it.

Technology has modified this last point. The recording arts attest to technology's impact on the performing arts. Film, musical recordings and tapes, compact discs, and videotape, permit audiences to respond long after the performances occurred. You may re-experience the recorded performance as often as you wish. However, even in these instances, a crucial difference separates the performing arts—live or recorded—from the visual/literary arts. This difference also makes the performing arts particularly compelling.

You solitarily experience novels, sculpture, or photography. Although you may experience the visual/literary arts with other people, a group is not essential for reading poetry or seeing a painting. You receive theatre, dance, or film as a member of an audience. The audience affects your response. Your individual response merges with all those watching the performance and forms an interactive link with the performers. The performing arts do not exist without audiences.

The performing arts are compelling because of their *immediacy*. Immediacy is the interaction between the performance—either live or recorded—and the audience, which is experiencing it in that same moment. Within the envelope of an auditorium two groups of human beings are experiencing simultaneously: artists are *doing* and audience members are *responding*. Immediacy is this simultaneous sharing of the artistic act and the responsive reaction.

Your memory of seeing a rock concert, a comedy played in a theatre, and a football or basketball game will illustrate the concept of immediacy. In all of these examples, the audience's positive response to the "action" of the event encourages the performers to their best abilities. A feedback loop exists between performer and audience. Action stimulates reaction: a funny line causes a laugh, which is an action that creates positive feelings in the performer. The cheers of a rock concert audience push the performers to *give* the audience even more to cheer about. Negative reactions—no applause, booing, no laughs at funny lines—will also affect performers. The immediacy of the performing arts stimulates *response*.

With film, recorded music, and videotape, the feedback loop is eliminated, but the audience will still respond to the performance *as if* it were happening *live*. Often we hear an audience applaud at the end of a film, or an album cut. We know the performers cannot hear. Yet the immediacy of the performance stimulates our honest emotional response. The visual/literary arts do not have this same immediacy. Immediacy makes the performing arts particularly compelling.

Audiences and the Performing Arts

If the performing arts are so compelling, why do people fail to support all of the performing arts? Film, TV, popular music, and radio have mass appeal with millions of us attending, watching, or listening. Theatre, opera, dance, and classical music appeal to approximately 6% of the United States population. Why the remarkable difference?

One reason is that the mass media present primarily popular entertainment, and the mass audience is interested in diversion and amusement. The other performing arts function more often as art; they encourage us to understand ourselves and our world; they provide perceptions that push our minds beyond the status quo into new and sometimes disturbing realms. For this reason the mass media will always remain overwhelmingly more popular than the live performing arts.

However, a second reason for the difference in popularity relates to our knowledge and experience. We have a vast knowledge and experience of TV, film, popular music, and radio; we may lack experience and knowledge of theatre, opera, dance, and classical music.

Radio and TV have been a part of our living from our earliest memories. Children start watching and listening as infants. These performing arts come into our living rooms, our bedrooms, and our cars at no cost. We have responded to them so often that we can function as serious critics of these media. Film is easily accessible; everyone has at least one movie theatre within an easy drive. We were introduced to movies as children by our parents; we continue to attend as an integral part of our social lives. The cost to attend films is reasonable. Popular music first enters our lives on the radio and through recordings. The next step—attendance at concerts—is a part of adolescence. The rock concert's importance as a social event tempers its high cost. Our growth to adulthood includes these performing arts as integral parts.

Our childhood and adolescent experiences with theatre, dance, opera, and classical music depend on a variety of factors. Where you live is important. Chicago, New York, Los Angeles, or any large city will have far more performing arts opportunities available than towns of 25,000 or less. In small towns the high school's performance activity may constitute the total experience in the performing arts. Also, parents' attitudes are important. Some parents actively encourage participation in performing arts events, taking their children to the theatre and filling their homes with the sounds of Beethoven and Mozart. The vast majority, however, have no active interest in the fine arts. Finally, the cost of the performing arts makes regular attendance difficult. In comparison with the mass media performing arts, theatre, dance, and classical music are scarcer, more expensive, and inconvenient to attend. Therefore, many of us accumulate little first-hand knowledge of these performing arts.

This lack of experience and knowledge may lead to negative attitudes that discourage attendance at the non-mass media performing arts. What are these attitudes?

Feelings of insecurity and stupidity may arise when you confront the idea of attending a ballet or symphony concert. What do I wear? To whom do I give my ticket? What door do I go in? What is going on? When do I applaud? What is supposed to be my reaction? These questions may cause you enough discomfort to stop the ticket purchase.

If we compare these feelings with your typical reactions to attending rock concerts or sporting events, we realize how knowledge and understanding are important. At a rock concert or football game you have no insecurities; you know "how to behave" and "how to react" to the concert or game. Your past experiences allow you to relax and enjoy all aspects of the experience.

However, knowledge and experience of these events do more than relieve potential insecurities. They allow you to evaluate the performance of the rock musician or football player. Because you have had previous experiences, you may compare and contrast this one with others. Because you may have seen them before or you know their music from their recordings, you are able to distinguish between the rock group playing at 50% of their potential and the group playing far beyond your wildest expectations. You can point out how the left-side of the offensive line caved in, allowing the quarterback to get sacked. These evaluations function as criticism.

Likewise, all responses to performing arts function as criticism. This criticism is merely your ability based on your experience and knowledge to distinguish "what works," "what doesn't work," and "why." Because you can really evaluate a lead guitarist's performance or a defensive tackle's, you enjoy the rock concert or the football game more. You appreciate the event. True appreciation derives from knowledge and experience, and the ability to evaluate.

How can you overcome fears and insecurities when facing some of the performing arts? Simply use the awarenesses derived from your comfortable involvement with the mass media and popular music. Fight insecurities with knowledge; fight fears with experience.

The study of the performing arts will increase your factual knowledge. However, attendance at performances must complement this information. By maximizing your experience and knowledge of the performing arts, you will increase your ability to evaluate them. From evaluation comes appreciation. With appreciation you start to enjoy the performing arts more.

KNOWLEDGE + EXPERIENCE ──────► ABILITY TO EVALUATE ──────► APPRECIATION

The Process of Experiencing the Performing Arts.

Performance Reaction Cards

We all have reactions to performances. These reactions function as criticism whether we like it or not. Good performance criticism needs to go beyond the simple "I liked it" response. Learning to make our reactions specific and detailed is an important first step in developing good performance criticism. The Performance Reaction Card assignment helps with these first steps.

Attend a performing arts event. On the Performance Reaction Cards included in this book answer these questions:

1. What really pleased you?
2. What did not "work" for you?
3. Which (if any) performers were especially effective or exciting and why?
4. What was your overall reaction to the event?

Make your responses as specifically detailed as possible; use details and examples from the performance. Explain your comments. The following example will illustrate a good reaction to a performance.

SAMPLE PERFORMANCE REACTION CARD

NAME _____

NAME OF EVENT: <u>Dance Concert</u>   PERFORMANCE DATE: _____

Respond in specific detail to the performance: 1) what really pleased you? 2) what did not "ork" for you? 3) which (if any) performers were especially effective/exciting and why? 4) what was your overall reaction to the event?

Since this was the first dance performance I'd ever attended, I was really pleased that it was a collection of dances rather than a single performance style. It provided me with the chance to fully experience many styles of the art of dance. I was actually overwhelmed with the talent of the dancers and the energy they presented.

I was, though, quite disappointed with the opening dance and was really worried that I was going to be completely turned off for the entire show. The concert opened with a ballet piece that was quite uninspiring. the dancers didn't really appear to be enjoying themselves which naturally left a poor impression on their audience. I also disliked the last piece which was done by a guest director, another ballet piece. (This is not to say I didn't enjoy any of the ballet pieces; I did.) I just got the impression from the dancers that they would much rather be performing jazz or some other modern style dance. Their movements seemed very mechanical.

My overall reaction to the 13 pieces of dance was one of enjoyment. I was continually intrigued by the dancers' expertise and the ease in which they carried out each movement. I am usually a left-brain-type of person, but my experience with the dance concert proved to be strictly right brain. I just sat back and let the chills run down my back as the street gang in ''The Higher You Rise'' rumbled in the alley with moves of modern dance. I laughed as the television commercial characters came to life during the theme song for ''Hawaii Five-O'' and ''The Days of Our Lives.'' Finally, I had to wonder if the ''Volunteer'' from the audience wasn't really a ''plant'' when ''Walkpeople'' did

(over)

its walking on stage. That volunteer seemed to have a natural talent. All in all, a very inspiring and intriguing event.

If Kathy Norris and Kent Lindener were embodied in their dance as much as the audience was, the stage would have been filled with tears. ''Heroes,'' a ballet done by a very talented and sensual couple had me feeling a sense of awe and wiping a tear from my cheek. I have never been so moved by one piece of art like their very sensual and sexual dance. They both danced individually, then together—reminding me of the boy-meets-girl and boy-gets-girl scenario—only this piece had an emotional twist. Kent left Kathy lying on the floor—melting in despair. He stopped just before going off stage and I could feel the audience feeling his want to take that last look, but he didn't. Instead, he left alone and left me wishing he would have come back or at least looked back once . . . a lost love, gone forever.

For my first experience with dance, I really enjoyed it and look forward to attending one againe in the near future!

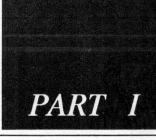

PART I

The Audience

Why do actors act? Singers sing? Dancers dance? Simple answer: applause. Applause shows approval, love, and acceptance of the performing artist's blood, sweat, and creativity. The source of applause is the audience, which is also the love/hate object for the performers. Their vocabulary about audiences reflects this:

"Let's go out and kill them" means the performers want to give an excellent performance.

"It's a good house tonight" means the audience is large and/or positively responsive—"They like us."

"It's a dead house tonight" means the audience is negatively responsive—"They don't like us."

Emotional reactions aside, performers know that without audiences their work would not exist. Audiences complete the crucial final link of the performance process.

Descriptions of Audiences

Audiences are so different. A general description would be impossible. Their specific natures are determined by the event, the background of the individual audience members, the experience of the performance, and the interactions among audience members. The following four descriptions illustrate how different audiences can be.

The huge 2,700 seat theatre was slowly filling as the 8 P.M. curtain time approached. Men dressed in suits and ties and women dressed in the latest fashions gave this occasion a "classy" feeling. The symphony members were coming onstage and beginning to tune up. The average age of the spectator was around 50; very few children were in attendance; no babies were seen or heard. Audience members socialized with friends over glasses of wine in the lobby; many continued to greet friends in the theatre itself after ushers had directed them to their reserve seats. As the house lights dimmed everyone hushed. The concert master entered to applause. The orchestra tuned one final time. We anticipated the beginning. A pause. A long silence. Then ... a burst of applause greeted the conductor. Soon the performance was underway.

An audience in the 2700 seat C.Y. Stephens Auditorium in Ames, IA (Courtesy of the Iowa State Center, Ames, IA.)

The 13,000 seat coliseum throbbed with noise, color, and energy as a capacity crowd pushed to fill the seats for this rock concert. The average age was 18; very few children under 10 were present; a few adults over 30 were noticed here and there. The audience's appearance ranged from informal to bizarre—levis, t-shirts, shorts, clothes imitating the group that was performing, and even make-up for both men and women. The noise was overwhelming. Some audience members secretly brought alcohol and marijuana, and were frantically drinking and smoking. A haze was starting to fill the vast arena. As the warm-up group entered to special lighting effects, the audience screamed and stood up. Many would remain standing on the floor or their seats throughout the performance.

The 200 seat movie theatre in the shopping mall was rapidly filling. It was Saturday night—"date night" for singles, a "night-out" for married couples. The 7 P.M. show was attracting both types of couples, plus a significant number of parents with children. Average age was about 21, probably due to the nature of the film—another episode of "Star Wars." Couples and groups were talking, eating popcorn and candy, and drinking soda pop. In fact, a rather active 10 year old had spilled his popcorn and drink, creating a mess that an usher was hurriedly working to clean as the previews began to flicker across the screen. Audience members continued to arrive, slowly and carefully walking down the center aisle and blocking the screen for many as they took whatever seats were available. As the feature started, a baby was crying loudly. Would the mother remove the child or would someone complain to an usher?

The young family rushed into the living room for the annual showing of "The Wizard of Oz." The kids were first to settle on the floor, except for 5 year old Susan who cuddled next to her Dad on the sofa. "Mom, hurry," Matt shouted to the kitchen. Everyone had a can of pop. As the familiar title played across the TV screen, Mom rushed in with the huge bowl of popcorn and several smaller bowls. As she settled in with Dad and Susan on the sofa, John, the 14 year old sauntered in, plopped into an armchair, and groaned: "Not 'Oz' again." A look from Dad silenced John as the TV showing of "Oz" began.

These four examples illustrate our varied experiences as audiences for the performing arts. If you were placed into any of the described audiences, your behavior would change remarkably depending on the nature of the audience, the experiences you were receiving from the performance, your background, and the quality of the interactions with the other audience members. The three chapters of Part I will explore this complexity of the audience experience.

Definition of Audience

An audience is a group of people assembled to experience a performance. Let's explore the definition.

"A group of people." We assemble in groups daily for a lot of different reasons. At school. At work. At home. At parties. We are familiar with groups and group behavior.

Interior of The Guthrie Theater showing the unique seven-sided thrust stage. The seating capacity is 1441 and no seat is more than 52 feet from the center of the stage. (Courtesy of the Gurthrie Theater, Minneapolis, MN Photography by Robert Ashley Wilson.)

Each of us modifies our behavior to adapt to the specific group that we are associating with. We behave differently with a group of friends or with fellow employees at work or with our family at a reunion.

A performing arts audience has its own nature. For the most part, it is a group of strangers, people who have come together but who do not know each other. Even if they know some audience members, very little social interaction occurs during the performance. The group is temporary. The duration of the performance defines the ''life'' of the audience. This group exists to experience the performance.

Within the audience are smaller groups with different purposes for being there. The following short list suggests some reasons why you may be a member of a performing arts audience.

1. You truly enjoy and love the art.
2. Your spouse/date truly enjoys the art.
3. You feel an obligation to support the arts.
4. You want to have a ''good time.''
5. You have nothing better to do.

6. You have to attend because of some class assignment.
7. You are entertaining a business client.
8. You are aware that it helps your social status to be "seen" at performing arts events.
9. You are using the performance as a social activity to be with friends or a date/spouse.
10. You want to see a specific performer.

As you can see, disparate groups compose any audience. We cannot simply say that an audience has one purpose in attending.

The intimate Maintenance Shop Theatre in the Memorial Union at Iowa State University, Ames, IA). (Courtesy of the Memorial Union. Photo by Mike Doolen.)

Interestingly, if a performance is engaging and exciting, these different purposes will coalesce as the performance happens. Individual purposes for attending are forgotten as audience members interact with the performance in the present moment of experiencing.

Their response becomes a complement to what the performers are doing. Performers and audience become as *one*.

Audiences come together to experience specific events. They "assemble to experience." These assembled experiences are individualized reactions to the performance and group interactions between you and the performers, and between you and other audience members. Understanding the basis for these reactions and interactions will expand the knowledge of your behavior as an audience member.

The Performing Arts and Communication

The performing arts communicate to audiences. This communication process is their reason for existing. Except for satisfying its creator, art that fails to communicate has no purpose. Since the performing arts need audiences to complete their artistic purpose, understanding the artistic communication process is important for audiences.

Our everyday communication practices differ from those in a performing arts setting. The simple, everyday model of human communication is well-known.

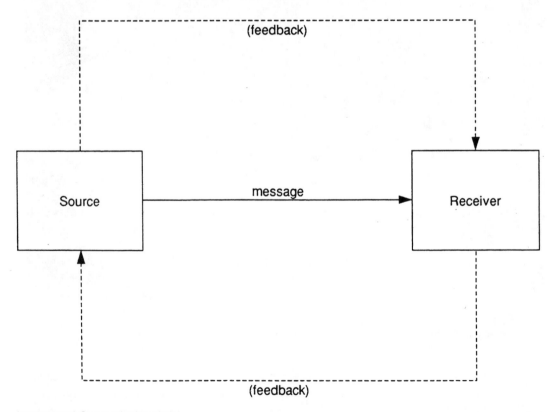

Interpersonal Communication Model.

The model illustrates the pattern for human communication. Think of a conversation with your best friend. As you talk to each other several essential elements of this communication model emerge.

1. *Direct communication.* You and your friend through verbal, aural, and visual stimuli speak directly to each other. Verbal stimuli are words; aural stimuli are sounds or noises, like "Uh,uh" or "Hmmm", which communicate meaning; visual stimuli are non-verbal body and facial language. In direct communication you may say anything that's on your mind and are reasonably sure that your ideas will be heard. You and your friend need no other person or technology for communication to take place.
2. *Maximal opportunities for feedback.* Feedback is reaction to what you have heard. In everyday conversation feedback opportunities are maximal. Nothing restricts the amount, quality, or intensity of your feedback. Also, because of the intimacy of the communication setting, you receive feedback from your friend with no restrictions.
3. *Communication is spontaneous.* Conversation is unplanned, even when you may have "rehearsed" what you want to say to a friend. Because we never know for sure what people will say to us, we are always creating the conversation in the present moment. Our everyday conversations are spontaneous.
4. *Communication pattern is "talk-listen".* The pattern that emerges from everyday communication is one of "talk," then "listen," "talk," then "listen." This pattern continues until the communication is complete.

Since communication is dynamic, all the elements in the model may be occurring simultaneously. You are listening or speaking, responding to or giving feedback, and processing the various stimuli bombarding your senses. As simple as the model looks, communication is a very complex act.

The performing arts communication model differs from the one for everyday communication. The generalized model on p. 22 will be made more specific for each of the performing arts we study.

Imagine yourself in a theatre responding to one of the performing arts. Elements of the performing arts communication model will distinguish themselves.

1. *Indirect communication.* You usually receive indirectly any communication in the performing arts. You observe characters in plays, films, and on television; you listen to music; you observe the kinetic movement of dancers. You cannot "talk" directly to any performers at the time of performance to clarify, to explain, or to react to their performances. The direct communication occurs on stage or on the screen; as an audience member you indirectly receive it through observation.
2. *Minimal and restrictive feedback opportunities.* Sitting in a theatre you have limited ways to express feedback to the performer. Applause, laughter, silence, program dropping, coughing, hissing, and booing will communicate to the performers your reactions. These feedback opportunities limit the range and subtlety of feed-

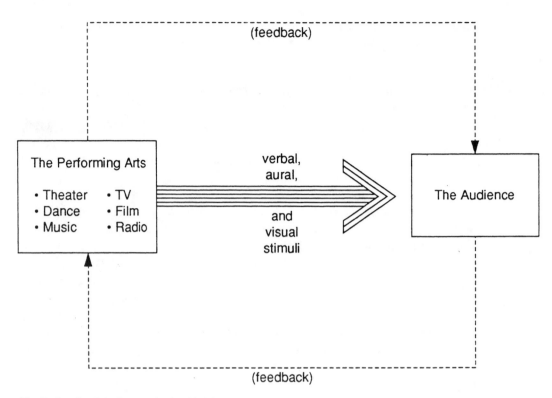

The Performing Arts Communication Model.

back communication. Only the extremes of pleasure and displeasure can impact the performers. Also, the "proper behavior" required by the formal settings of theatre, dance, and classical music events restrict feedback. With television, film, and radio, the feedback loop is incomplete since the performers are not present when the event is received.

3. *Communication is planned and rehearsed.* Contrasting with the everyday situations, performing arts communication is not spontaneous. All the arts extensively plan and rehearse what will be shared with the audience. Although theatre, dance, and music performances vary slightly from night to night and intensify from the rehearsals, major changes seldom occur. Film and video tape processing fix forever most television and film performances.

4. *Communication pattern is "listen-listen"* . As an audience member you have one basic activity: to listen to the performing art. Listening includes both receiving aural stimuli (those stimuli that affect hearing) and visual stimuli (those that affect sight). The environment and the activity restricts your opportunities to "talk." If you talk, other audience members may complain; you may be removed from the

theatre. Even the environments of more informal performing arts discourage your talking. The basic communication pattern is to listen.

Audience Feedback as Interaction

As mentioned earlier, the nature of feedback in the two communication models differs. Although the feedback during a performance is limited, it uniquely functions in the creation of the performance.

The performer needs an audience. Without an audience the performer's art is nonexistent. However, the audience serves as more than the final connection in a communication model or as more than a passive receiver—a cup into which performers pour their art. The audience's immediate responses—its limited feedback—stimulates the performers to performance excellence. How does this happen?

Audience feedback creates a special interaction between performer and audience:

> The musical performer begins her big comic song. As the song progresses the audience laughs; the performer becomes more excited and energized. Her performance surpasses rehearsals. The audience is roaring with laughter. She responds with pleasure and creativity. The audience breaks in often with applause. The number ends with cheers and an ovation.

This example illustrates interaction and how feedback functions as its crucial component. As the audience reacts to the performer, the performer reacts immediately to the stimulus of the audience's feedback. Reciprocal reactions continue until the performance ends. The audience's reactions can be positive or negative. However, whatever they are, the reactions will be received and responded to.

The *social contagion theory* explains why this special sharing between performer and audience occurs. People in groups tend to react in the same ways; behavior in groups in contagious among the people in the groups, i.e., it's "catching." Therefore when the audience gets excited so do the performers. However, group behavior is also contagious among the audience members. Social contagion theory accounts for your laughing aloud more at a funny film when you are in a large audience than when you see the same movie alone.

Will this interaction happen in television, radio, and film where time and space separates the audience and performers? The nature of the performing art modifies the quality and amount of the interaction, but interaction is certainly present. Most often the impact of the response to the performance will be delayed. The performers discover the audience's pleasure or displeasure by the size of the A.C. Neilsen television ratings or by the weekly gross ticket sales for a movie. Knowing that time and space separates them from their audiences, television and radio performers attempt more personal methods in presentation. Newscasters speak directly to the camera so that it appears they are talking specifically to you, and radio announcers talk to the microphone as if it were a real person. Among audience members the interaction is the same for film as it is for the live performing arts. Comedy series on television are performed before live audiences or use "laugh tracks" to stimulate the at-home audience to respond as a live theatre audience.

Interaction between audience and performer affects the performance in positive or negative ways. Interaction among audience members enhances the nature of the response. These phenomena illustrate the social contagion theory at work in the performing arts.

The "Language" of Communication

The "language" of communication differs between the two communication models. We need no instruction in the language of the everyday communication model; we have learned it—both the aural and visual components—as we have matured, and as we practice it daily. However, the "languages" of the performing arts need to be learned as we learned the elements of English and the nuances of non-verbal communication. Part of your learning about the performing arts will focus on understanding the basic elements of the "language" used to communicate the values and meaning of each art.

Too often audiences assess communication in the performing arts context using the criteria of the language used in our daily communication. As an example, theatre seems merely observed conversation. However, to evaluate theatre using only the "language" of everyday communication would cause you to miss much of theatre's unique "language".

Audiences also may erroneously use the language of one performing art to evaluate another. Film and theatre appear so similar that we often use our knowledge of film's language of communication to judge a theatre performance. Your participation as a audience member depends on learning the languages of the performing arts.

You and the Performing Arts

As an audience member you have an important responsibility to be an active participant in the creative activity that you are experiencing. As an active participant you need to understand:

1. What you bring as an audience member every time that you attend a performance.
2. How you respond to a performance, i.e., how your brain receives and assimilates the stimuli of a performance, and how interactions with other audience members affect your response.
3. How you can enhance your response to the performing arts, i.e., specific actions and behaviors which will increase your enjoyment of performances.

The following chapters will address each of these points. After reading them you will have a more complete picture of the complex role an audience member plays in the performing arts communication process.

CHAPTER 1

What Do You Bring to the Performing Arts?

The audience, the crucial link in the performing arts communication model, completes the artistic/creative act initiated by performers. As the completing connection, audiences also provide significant feedback, which stimulates the performer and the audience itself.

As important as its group behavior is, we must remember that individuals make up audiences. Each individual brings different backgrounds and experiences to the event. These include any involvement with or knowledge of the performing arts, as well as life experiences that influence how you feel about a performing art. Because what you bring to a performance will affect how you respond, understanding the considerable information and attitudes that you hold already toward the performing arts will give you a basis for further growth and development.

Background

We come from a variety of backgrounds. Cultural, ethnic, family, educational, economic, and social differences define our unique natures. These backgrounds affect how we perceive the world and how we interpret any experience in life. They influence our perceptions and interpretations of the performing arts. In other words, based on your background, you enter a theatre with definite attitudes toward a performance before you even experience it.

Let's examine a hypothetical example: attending a performance of the popular Christmas-time ballet "The Nutcracker Suite" from three different persons' perspectives.

CULTURAL		
A *(FEMALE)*	*B* *(MALE)*	*C* *(MALE)*
Excited about the performance. Both attends and studies ballet for 10 years. Also attends theatre and symphony concerts.	Has mixed feelings about performance. Only six live dance experiences in his background. Has childhood memories of "Nutcracker" attendance with Mom.	Hates the idea of attending. Only attends movies and watches TV. Likes sports events and rock concerts.

ETHNIC		
Black American	Dad: Hispanic Mom: Irish Catholic American	White Anglo-Saxon Protestant

FAMILY		
Parents have supported and encouraged interest in the arts	Dad: never attends performances unless "dragged." Mom: loves the arts and has taken son to arts events.	Parents are not involved arts, except as social events.

SOCIAL		
Friends attend and practice all the arts—both visual and performance.	Male friends think dancers are sissies. Girl friend studies dance. Most of her friends like dance.	No friends have been involved in dance. Date wanted to go.

EDUCATION		
College Sophomore	College Sophomore	College Sophomore

ECONOMIC		
Upper-middle class Loans and parents are paying for college.	Lower-middle class Loans, grants, and work are paying for college.	Upper-class Parents are paying for college.

As you can imagine, A, B, and C will respond to "The Nutcracker" in different ways. Their backgrounds will be determining factors. Whatever happens during the ballet will be filtered through attitudes and beliefs that they will bring to the theatre. Imagine the various backgrounds that are part of any audience. A significant part of your response to any performing art has nothing to do with the performance itself. Previous attitudes and beliefs influence our reactions to the event.

A final point: human experience is fluid and changeable. We all have the potential to modify parts of our backgrounds, especially those parts open to change in the present, i.e., cultural, social, educational, and economic. Our "pasts" alone need not determine our attitudes toward the performing arts. Experience and information in the present may provoke changes, which will reshape our backgrounds toward performances.

Listening Experience

As defined earlier, listening in the performing arts includes receiving both aural and visual stimuli. Listening, a complex behavior, involves all our senses. It encompasses more than what passes through our ears. Although we listen each day of our lives, listening as a part of an audience presents different demands than our usual daily experiences. What are the components of the performing arts listening experience?

Performing arts listening is a *group experience*. Most often a person responds to the performing arts as a member of a group. And, as discussed earlier, the nature of how we respond will be influenced by the group's behavior. Unfortunately most of our group listening is associated with sitting in classrooms for 12 to 16 years.

The positive and negative behaviors we have learned from classroom listening may initially transfer to the audience experience. Classroom listening has taught us how to remain attentive over relatively long periods of time; how to engage ourselves with the instructor and with our fellow classmates; how to concentrate. However, we have also learned how to *look* attentive and *do* and *think* about other things; how to escape boring instructors or lessons through daydreaming; how to focus on the most insignificant distractions.

Each audience member has *different purposes for attending*. The assumption that an audience has a single unified purpose for attending—to respond to the performance—ignores the reasons people attend any performance. Our purposes for being in the audience impact our listening. They affect our attention to the performance and our interest in listening. If you listen with less attention and interest, you reduce the chances that the performance will make its desired aesthetic impression.

Performing arts listening occurs in a *restrictive communication environment*. Sitting in a theatre with other people restricts the freedom of your response to what you see and hear. The group discourages verbal response among audience members or with performers. Other audience members may quiet anyone who disturbs the performance by talking. Therefore, you have little opportunity to respond verbally, an uncomfortable condition from some people. The audience's situation offers even more restrictions than the classroom listening.

Performing arts listening emphasizes *physical passivity*. Audience members of theatre, dance, and music performances (excluding most popular music events) have little opportunity to move. The formal theatre environment and group expectations encourage *listening while sitting.* Only extraordinary emergencies permit leaving the theatre during a performance.

This physical passivity contrasts with the freedom of movement allowed with the more informal performing arts. At a rock concert you feel free to stand and shout, dance in the aisles, or even stand on the seats. The rock performance stimulates this activity and the whole audience participates actively. As you watch a film in a theatre, you can get up and leave for more popcorn at any time. This action is accepted by other audience members and encouraged by the theatre management, who show commercials promoting ''Have a snack'' and inform audiences that the snack bar is closing in five minutes.

Even greater informality exists with television and radio listening; viewers move whenever and wherever they please during these performance events. Since your performance models for listening behavior are the informal performing arts, you may feel uncomfortable and limited in an audience of the more formal performing arts. This physical passivity affects your listening.

The listeners to the performing arts have a *shortened attention span.* Most audience members have an attention span for sitting and listening to the performing arts that is significantly shorter than our ancestors'. Audiences even as recently as the 1950's expected Broadway plays lasting at least two and one-half hours, attended double bills at the movies, or listened to the radio for 3–4 hours in the evening. Around 1900 audiences felt cheated if their theatre evening was not a 4–5 hour experience, which might include an orchestral overture and between-act music, a full-play, variety acts, and a short play as an after-piece. Why has our attention spans for the performing arts shortened?

Our individual tempo-rhythms, i.e., our internal responses to time, reflect the pace of our technological society. Information speeds around the world in seconds; at work computers process information in milli-seconds; we even expect restaurants to serve our food to be served *fast* and *on demand.* We even have less patience with performing arts which do not engage us immediately.

With entertainment we have developed concentrated attention spans of eight to twelve minutes from our watching television since childhood. The average American spends over seven and one-half hours each day watching television. This television experience teaches us to concentrate on the performance only eight to twelve minutes. Longer concentration is impossible, because commercials interrupt the performance. Television does not permit focusing on the performance for longer time periods. Therefore, we develop naturally a shortened attention span for the performing arts from the very influential early years of childhood before anyone has any experiences in theatres. Because of the short attention span, theatre performances of two hours, broken only with one intermission, may seem unbearably long. They strain an audience member's concentration. This shortened attention affects how you listen and therefore how you *receive* the performance.

The performing arts experience places new demands on your listening skills. Your listening techniques must adjust to performance situations. New approaches to listening must develop. These adjustments and chances will enhance your reception of the performing arts, and ultimately increase your enjoyment and appreciation.

An Individual's Experience with the Performing Arts

Everytime you attend a performance, you bring along your accumulated experiences with that performing art. As each person in an audience is unique, likewise each person's experiences with performing arts vary. Some audience members will have attended many performances; some will be attending for the first time. How does this variation in experience affect audience response?

The greater your experience the greater the likelihood that you will involve yourself in the aesthetic elements of performance. Aesthetic involvement increases the range and intensity of your reactions. These reactions feed back directly to performers and your fellow audience members. If your experience is limited, the range and intensity of your aesthetic involvement with the performance will decrease, which affects feedback.

If intense aesthetic appreciation require knowledge and experience, how can the exuberant reactions of first-time viewers of any performance be explained? If you remain open to receiving any new experience, you have the potential of being caught up in its energy, excitement, and aesthetic. "Remaining open" in the performing arts usually means allowing your right brain to receive the experience, and avoiding left brain impulses to evaluate. Even a first-time viewer of ballet will be captured by the movement, the spectacle, the beauty of the performers, and the music without understanding the intricacies of ballet choreography. More information about the interactions between right and left brain in receiving the performing arts follows in the next chapter.

As we experience more performances of any art our aesthetic appreciation grows. We walk into performances more knowledgeable, ready to respond emotionally and thoughtfully. Accumulating performance experiences may reduce our right brain responses to the immediacy of the performance. We could become left-brain cognitive evaluators of the arts. Be wary. Remember: our first pleasures in the arts were right brain—intuitive, spontaneous, simultaneous, non-verbal. No matter how many experiences we may have, we must never lose this way into appreciating performance.

Imagination

We all have the mental ability to imagine; imagination is part of our mind's capacity. We have all heard:

- "She's got a wonderful imagination"
- "Only with his imagination could she have created such a work of art."
- "It's only your imagination"

What is imagination? Imagination is the mind's capacity to form ideal or fictional images of things that are not actually present to the senses. On the coldest day in January when you close your eyes and create the image of a sunny beach and respond to the feelings of warmth, you are using your imagination.

Some of us did not give up the imaginative play of childhood just because adults urged us to be "big boys and girls." As we grew up we translated the reality of child's play to the imagination. We created mental images of ideal worlds, fictional situations, or fantastic experiences. Imagination is a crucial mental capacity for all people, but especially for artists and scientists. Without this ability to see beyond the reality of the senses, no significant scientific or artistic achievement is possible.

The socialization process from childhood to adolescence to adulthood often stifles imaginative growth. The process of becoming an "acceptable" member of a group pressures us to leave behind "childlike" activity and conform to the group's norms of behavior. Eccentricity of any sort is shunned. Any imaginative activity, e.g., game-playing, is discarded; new norms emphasize reality-based activities. Any use of the imagination is relegated to moments alone. However, these moments become less and less, as "group" activities gain prominence. Being alone becomes intolerable to many. As moments to imagine freely become reduced, imagination may atrophy, i.e., waste away, from disuse.

Our educational system may unintentionally suppress the imaginations of young people. Students are rewarded for activities that are "reality-based." Imagination seems only stimulated in art, music, and creative drama classes, which meet far less often than "reality-based" classes in English, mathematics, science, and social studies. The system emphasizes that imagination is not practical or significant. The grading systems reward the pragmatic realist rather than the imaginative idealist.

The performing arts exercise your imagination. They stretch your present capability to imagine through the performance experience. Bombarded by sensory stimuli your imagination replenishes its store. Any of the performing arts can cause this growth—a film, a stage play, a dance concert, a symphony concert, or television drama. A creative imagination increases your enjoyment of the performing arts and enriches your everyday lives.

Conclusion

As you are now aware, you bring a great deal to a performance. No matter what your experience with the performing arts is, your life experiences will cause you to respond to a performance in certain ways. The next step in your audience knowledge is understanding how you respond to a performance. With that information you will understand how your past (what you bring to a performance) interacts with the present (how you respond to a performance) to affect the future (your growth in responding to the performing arts).

CHAPTER 2

How Do You Respond to the Performing Arts?

Our minds are always thinking. We take in, process, store, and respond to a variety of stimuli each day. Our sensory centers in our brain are constantly adjusting and responding to sensory stimuli. Our memories store important facts, information, and emotions consciously and unconsciously. Our left and right hemispheres process stimuli in different ways, but their processing is all a part of whole brain thinking.

Our thinking is always with us, but, as Kenneth Atchity in *A Writer's Time* asserts, we resist it:

> Most of us hate to think. Five minutes of thought can be more terrifying, more energy-draining than days and days of routine or habitual activity. Your mind is intrinsically thrifty, and prefers to do things the way it has done them before. It sees its primary business as establishing effective channels for action, and resists altering a channel that has become established, to say nothing of constructing a new one that cause anxiety. (p.3)

We choose familiar performance experiences—the same kinds of movies, TV programs, and/or music—to avoid thinking and to maintain our routines. However, as audience members we must learn to think effectively for real engagement in the performing arts experience.

An audience receives a variety of stimuli during a performance. The performing arts communication model suggests visual, verbal, and aural stimuli impact on our conscious and unconscious minds. These stimuli differ depending on the "language" of the art being experienced. How do our minds process the information collected during a performance?

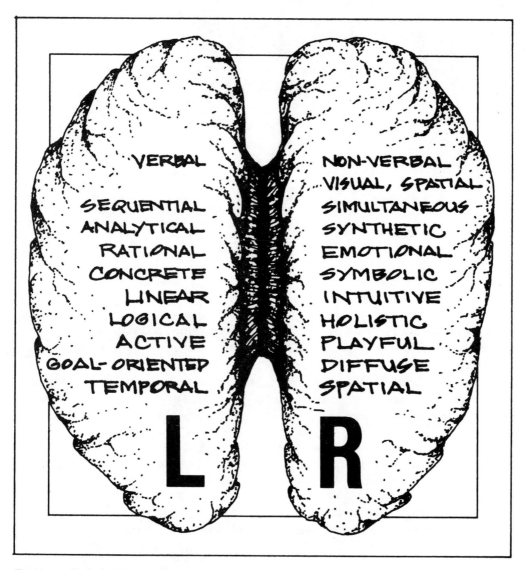

The Human Brain: Left/Right Hemispheres (Illustration by Fritz Szabo.)

Left Brain, Right Brain, and the Performing Arts

The human brain is divided into two hemispheres connected by the corpus collasum, which connects the two hemispheres and allows for interaction between the two.

Although the interaction between the two hemispheres is cooperative and complementary, the two hemispheres contrast in *how* they process information. Some differences have been noted in patients whose hemispheres have been surgically divided; other differences are more speculative. The following chart describes the distinctions between the two hemispheres in regard to ways of thinking.

Left Hemisphere	Right Hemisphere
Verbal	Nonverbal, visual-spatial
Sequential	Simultaneous
Analytical	Synthetic
Rational	Emotional
Concrete	Symbolic
Linear	Intuitive
Logical	Holistic
Active	Playful
Goal-oriented	Diffuse
Temporal	Spatial

The distinctions in the chart illustrate how each hemisphere processes the visual and aural stimuli coming into the brain. The verbal-nonverbal distinction, having emerged from considerable research with split-brain patients and normal subjects, is the least speculative of the distinctions. Sally P. Springer and George Deutsch in their book *Left Brain, Right Brain* clarify one of the other distinctions:

> The sequential-simultaneous distinction reflects a current though not universally accepted, theoretical model holding that the left hemisphere tends to deal with rapid changes in time and to analyze stimuli in terms of details and features, while the right hemisphere deals with simultaneous relationships and with more global properties of patterns. (p. 185)

The logical-holistic distinction focuses on the left hemisphere's ability to break down experiences into their component parts (analytical) and to understand other parts in logical, ordered terms. The right hemisphere treats experience as an unified whole which has a reality independent of and greater than the sum of its parts (holistic) and looks to bring together stimuli (synthetic) rather than break them down into component parts.

How does left brain/right brain distinctions affect our audience experience of the arts? In various significant ways. Let's first consider what kind of stimuli each performing art primarily provides and what side of the brain is primarily influenced:

Performing Art	Left-Hemisphere	Right Hemisphere
Film, theatre, TV, radio (drama)	Aural	Visual-Aural
Dance		Aural-Visual
Music		Aural-Visual

The performing arts significantly use right hemisphere activity, or ''R-mode thinking.''[1]

Dance and music especially stimulate right hemisphere activity. As you respond to a popular music group, you are not analyzing the experience in sequential terms, making logical sense of all the musical and visual stimuli, in an attempt to verbalize your response. Not at all! The music's aural stimuli are processed as a simultaneous experience with the visual and spatial patterns created by the performers, their costumes, lighting, and special effects. A rock concert, like any music or dance performance, is a holistic experience, i.e., an experience understood as a whole and not by its individual parts.

Even the drama in theatre, film, and television involves the right hemisphere through dramatic action, characters, and visual stimuli that go beyond its usual patterns of logical plotting and sequential development of character. Dramatic action can flashback or flash-forward in time; film drama may use dream sequences that have no basis in real time; TV drama can take you to different worlds that you have never imagined; and radio drama is imaginative fantasy at its maximum as you exercise the right brain to create visions of action and character created only by aural stimuli. These experiences demand an ability to utilize R-mode thinking.

The right brain actively processes the non-verbal stimuli from any drama production. The visual stimuli include design elements: the appropriate mood lighting; the use of color in set, costumes, and lighting; the actual form and dimension of costumes and set. Actors' physicalizations in performance communicate visually: the posture, walk, and gestures delineate psychological and physical dimensions of a character; eye focus and facial gesture communicate nonverbal messages; a caress on the cheek or a slap in the face speak without verbal support.

R-mode processing is even used in reacting to an actor's handling of the text. Words have denotative and connotative meanings. The denotative meaning, or dictionary definition, conveys only part of a word's meaning. Its emotional, or connotative meaning, in the theatre is the actor's responsibility. Actors vocally color words with emotion. The audience will perceive the varying vocal tones and inflections. Thomas R. Blakeslee in his book *The Right Brain* asserts:

> The left brain generally responds to the literal meaning of the words it hears and will not even notice the meaning of inflection. The right brain perceives different aspects of the same conversation: tone of voice, facial expression, and body language are noticed while the words are relatively less important. (p. 28)

To respond to an actor's performance means true holistic listening, i.e., listening verbally and nonverbally.

The right brain synthesizes these visual, aural, and nonverbal stimuli into patterns, allowing the audience to intuit conclusions about the dramatic action, characters, or meaning

---

1. I am indebted to Betty Edwards' *Drawing on the Right Side of the Brain* and *Drawing on the Artist Within* for introducing me to this concept.

The Right Brain At Work! (Dillon reprinted by permission: Tribune Media Services.)

of a play. The right brain will combine the actor's body language and vocal inflections into a meaningful whole, and will integrate that with the visual influences of design occurring at that moment. Audiences must develop their R-mode thinking to receive the maximum impact of the performance of drama in theatre, film, or television.

How you utilize your brain in responding to the performing arts will affect the quality of the experience. The majority of people in western civilization are highly left hemisphere dominant. Our culture and education have encouraged and stimulated our left brain dominance. In the performing arts the left brain insists on analyzing the experience as it is happening. Based upon its cumulative experience the left brain wants to evaluate the acting, music, or dance; the director's choices in theatre, film, or television; and the design elements based upon its cumulative experience. L-mode thinking wants to actively control your response to performances.

All the performing arts encourage, if not demand, right brain processing of sensations. You can consciously expand your right brain capability as you attend the theatre, concerts, films, or watch television.

Cognitive and Emotional Reactions in the Performing Arts[2]

We all have unique experiences in reacting to and reacting with performances. A film audience watching the same emotionally wrenching scene might respond to it in various ways. If the scene were in a hospital where a young mother dying of cancer is making a tearful goodbye to her two young sons and is encouraging their strength and obedience to their father, the following are possible responses:

---

2. I am indebted to Dr. Mark Redmond, Associate Professor of Speech Communication, Iowa State University, for introducing me to these concepts that explain the cognitive and emotional reactions of all human communication.

35

I felt very sorry for the mother. She was so young to die. I felt uncomfortable with all the crying.

The scene was dumb. I don't like scenes that are sad. I just refused to watch.

Like the mother I thought that her children needed to be strong and to do what their Dad told them in the future.

No, I'm not a mother, but I could tell that she was trying to be so positive with her kids. She was trying not to cry in front of her kids.

I felt with the kids. I saw myself standing next to a hospital bed with my Mom in it. I became over- whelmed with grief. I couldn't stop crying.

These reactions are honest and sincere. Some show greater emotional response; others illustrate a more cognitive response. Our familiarity with, sensitivity to, and perception of the performing arts will influence our reactions.

You will have a response to any performance. If you react *to* a performance, you remain an objective observer commenting on the action. If you react *with* a performance, you become involved in the action yourself; by taking an active role in the experience, you put yourself into the situation of the performance. "Reacting to" is a reactive process of evaluating experience from your own perspective. "Reacting with" is a proactive process of understanding experience from another person's viewpoint, or from the aesthetic perspective.

Three types of reactions are possible:

1. affective: involving your emotions or feelings.
2. cognitive: involving your thoughts or ideas.
3. physical: involving physical reactions of your body.

During performances the aesthetic experience and aesthetic pleasure require reacting with. Both reactive and proactive responses participate in critical evaluation. Examples on p. 37 will clarify these terms.

As you watch a performance you naturally shift between "reacting to" and "reacting with." At times they are happening simultaneously as you receive and respond to the stimuli of the performance. Likewise you may simultaneously be responding cognitively, emotionally, and physically. Our minds naturally "make sense" of all of this complexity and do so unconsciously. Usually you do not rationally control this process.

Understanding how you respond may increase your abilities to react with. You enter performances with your present capability to empathize. The performance experience, which is primarily responsive rather than action-oriented, allows *conscious* expansion of your ability to empathize by involving you *consciously* in the worlds of other people. Our empathy can grow and develop if given the opportunity. The performing arts provide a safe, comfortable environment to increase empathy.

AFFECTIVE

REACTING TO	*REACTING WITH*
"Sympathy" is the reaction, i.e., you feel sorrow or pity; you cognitively share the feelings of the performer/character.	"Empathy" is the reaction, i.e., you accept the performer's/character's feelings *as your own;* they evoke the memory of your own experience.
Cognitive/emotional act	Imaginative/emotional act
"I felt very sorry for the mother. She was so young to die. I felt uncomfortable with all the crying."	"I felt with the kids. I saw myself standing next to a hospital bed with my Mom in it. I became overwhelmed with grief. I couldn't stop crying."

COGNITIVE

The performance stimulates you to think about the experience from a self-centered perspective; you analyze the performance from your own point of view.	The performance stimulates you to think about the experience from the performer's/character's perspective; you analyze the person's perspective from the cognitive point of view. "Cognitive empathy" is the reaction.
Cognitive act	Cognitive act
"The scene was dumb. I don't like scenes that are sad. I just refused to watch."	"Like the mother I thought that her children needed to be strong and to do what their Dad told them in the future."

PHYSICAL

A physical response caused by an ego-centered reaction to the performance.	A physical response caused by an empathic reaction to the performance.
Physical act	Physical act
Closing your eyes during a bloody, violent scene.	Recoiling in shock or surprise as a person jumps out from the darkness.

Also, as your empathy grows so will your appreciation for the arts. Your ability to empathize involves you with a performance. Your aesthetic pleasure, i.e., the pleasure you derive from the performing art, depends on your experiences and abilities to react with. Much of our aesthetic pleasure in theatre, film, and TV is empathic.

How can you increase your empathy? Let's return to the affecting scene of a mother dying of cancer saying good-bye to her two children. One response was: "This scene is dumb. I don't like scenes that are sad. I just refused to watch." This response is cognitive "reacting to." To develop your "reacting with" you only need to watch and listen. If you honestly concentrated on the scene, your present human capability to empathize would cause you to identify or fantasize with the kids or the mother. You would start to feel in their place, maybe even start to cry. The conscious action needed to empathize begins with actively listening to the performance. Honest concentrated listening opens the right hemisphere of your brain to sensations and emotions. Active concentration on sensations and emotions fills the mind, and prevents the left hemisphere from imposing order and logic in the present moment.

What better place to explore empathy than in a theatre? Even though hundreds cf people surround you, they are paying no attention to your emotional responses. They are caught up in their own feelings. A theatre is a really safe place to expand your empathy.

If you allow cognitive and affective empathy, emotion and tears to happen, what are the results? First, you expand your ability to "react with," an ability useful in responding not only to the performing arts but also in everyday life. Growth in understanding the thoughts and feelings of other people expands our "selves" and our abilities to interact with others. Secondly, through empathy you understand the performers and their art better. This aesthetic understanding expands your experience and knowledge of the art and thereby increases your ability to appreciate it. Only through cognitive and affective empathy can we as audience members really involve ourselves in the performing arts. And, finally, this experience opens you to empathy as a process; then the next opportunity to "react with" may be easier.

Responding in an Audience: Important Audience Interactions

As audience members receiving the stimuli of the performing arts experience, we are simultaneously involved with important audience interactions which affect how we respond to a performance. Understanding these interactions will enhance a performance's impact on your senses.

The *social contagion theory* has been discussed already as part of the feedback phenomenon in the performing arts communication model. Knowing that people in groups tend to behave in similar ways reveals how our limited feedback stimulates performers to their highest levels and our fellow audience members to their peak responses. Therefore, audience members should be active participants in the performance, not passive receivers. Feedback is an important audience responsibility precisely because it has a dynamic affect on performance.

Aesthetic vs. Social Experience of the Performance

Every performance that we attend has an aesthetic and social dimension. In fact the experience of the performance will include both. A good performance involves you more completely in the aesthetic experience, but never can you avoid the social dimension.

The aesthetic experience is the product of the performance, the special world created by the performance. The aesthetic dimension includes all the elements of the performing art being watched. It is simply the audience's relationship to the performers and their arts; this relationship goes beyond their existence as human beings.

The social experience is the audience's awareness of the performers and other audience members as human beings existing within the same social and physical environment. The social dimension includes awarenesses of the theatre building, the comfort of the seats, other audience members, and the performers as they exist separate from their art.

To clarify these concepts, let's create the beginning moments of a theatre performance and identify the aesthetic and social experience in action.

A Night at the Theatre: The Aesthetic And the Social

As you enter the auditorium you are struck by its intimacy; only about 400 seats and none are more than 50 feet from the stage. "Great," you think, "no problems seeing or hearing tonight."

While the usher shows you and your date to your seats, both of you recognize people in the audience and wave. Settling into the seat you respond to its firm comfort and note how the seats all have different color fabrics in alternating patterns. "Neat." An older man and his wife sit next to you; you nod and smile even though you do not know them. [These are all part of the social experience]

You suddenly become aware of the set onstage. "No curtain hiding the set. That's different," you share with your date. As you stare at the stage, you notice the massive shapes and form of the set design. With the highly shadowed lighting, the whole set gives off a mysterious, eerie mood; you feel like something dangerous could happen up there. [You are starting to involve yourself in the aesthetic experience]

" How long do you think the play will last?"

"Hunh?"

"How long do you think the play will last!?"

"Oh...I don't know. A couple hours." [This question from your date brings you back to the social experience of the performance.]

The house lights dim. The audience gets quiet, as some very somber but disquieting music refocuses your attention to the mysterious set. The house lights go out. You sit in the dark listening to this music now complemented by weird voices. As the lights slowly rise, you see three witches sitting around a cauldron. [You are starting again to involve yourself in the aesthetic experience]

"That's Barbara from my English class," you think. "I didn't know she was interested in acting." [The social experience of the performance returns]

The first act of *Macbeth* continues and after 25 minutes, you are really involved in the play's action and characters. [Aesthetic experience] Suddenly the man next to you sneezes, and you become very much aware that he has a bad cold. [Social experience] As you think about how to avoid his germs, you notice that you have missed the entrance of a new character. You start to focus in again on the play.

During any performance you move between the social and aesthetic experience. Being aware of these two aspects of a performance will allow you to develop techniques, many of them R-mode thinking, to increase your involvement with the aesthetic experience.

Willing Suspension of Disbelief

For audience members to accept the aesthetic experience of any performance, they must actively choose it. An act of individual will power accepts the aesthetic experience in place of the "real world" and its social reality. We willingly suspend our disbelief in order to involve ourselves in the world of the performance.

This act of will that gives up the social experience in favor of the aesthetic experience operates in all the performing arts, but especially in the performance of drama. We know that the flickering images on the film screen are not real. However, for the duration of the film we suspend our disbelief and involve ourselves in the world of the film. We believe in characters, action, and plot as fantastic as those in the *Star Wars* movies. This suspension of disbelief allows us to engage ourselves with the performance and to enjoy the results of the creative work. Although we do not always have to create belief in fictional worlds to enjoy a music or dance concert, we must give ourselves over to the worlds of the musicians and dancers. We must give up the social experience of performance.

Both left and right brain are active when you suspend disbelief. The left brain allows suspension of disbelief to happen. Relinquishing control of disbelief is a left brain action. Once the left brain permits you to give up the social experience and your preoccupation with the "real world," you can open both the right and left brain to experiencing the performance. You become involved in the performance both cognitively and emotionally by the act of willingly suspending disbelief.

Willing suspension of disbelief encourages our abilities to "react with." Only by giving up the social in favor of the aesthetic experience will cognitive and affective empathy happen during a performance. If you never willingly suspend disbelief, you will remain actively "reacting to" and evaluating, which precludes your entering the world of the performance.

Aesthetic Distance

Despite the importance of our emotional and cognitive involvement in the performance's aesthetic experience, audience members must separate themselves from the performance for certain kinds of emotional responses to occur. During a play performance audience members must be involved with the characters, but without taking action. As you watch the murderer creeping behind the victim sitting on the sofa, you feel the emotional tension of the dramatic action, but you also do not leap from your seat to save the victim. At the same time you are involved emotionally in the performance and you remain detached and separated from it. If your seat is too close to or too far from a performance's action, you feel the impact of aesthetic distance. Too close to the action may destroy the aesthetic reality and willing suspension of disbelief; too far from the action may prohibit the aesthetic dimension from engaging due to the prominence of the social experience. This mental/physical separation or detachment is called aesthetic distance.

Aesthetic distance assists our involvement in the performing arts. The proper aesthetic distance allows us to become emotionally involved in what we know is fictitious and even unbelievable. Aesthetic distance allows us to experience the most awe-inspiring or the most terrible without needing to take action.

This left-brain function naturally develops during our experiencing of the performing arts. Children have little sense of aesthetic distance. In viewing a performance of *Hansel and Gretel,* children often try to stop the witch from popping Hansel and Gretel into the oven. The children act, because they can not yet distinguish between the aesthetic and social experience of performances. In our lifetimes we experience thousands of terrifying events in theatres, and because of aesthetic distance have learned to integrate the terror and excitement into our aesthetic not social sensiblities.

Sometimes performers destroy our aesthetic distance. Mental separation between you and musicians can be eliminated if the sounds of the music are too loud; much contemporary music in performance is painful listening for adults, destroying (or, for young people, enhancing) aesthetic distance. Some audience members have aesthetic distance destroyed by nudity in the theatre or dance. Also, if performers break the usual physical separation between themselves and audience, e.g., actors who leave the stage during a performance and confront audience members in their seats, aesthetic distance may be destroyed.

Some performance groups *consciously* choose to break the usual aesthetic constraints of a performing art. When these occasions happen, the performance group or artist wants to encourage a different or new sensibility toward performance, and therefore tries to shatter the usual conventions that exist between artist and performer. Theatre performances sometimes bring actors into the audience. The audience's aesthetic distance is destroyed; performers become other human beings not characters in a play, which affects the communication between the performers and the audience. Such circumstances reduce empathy and increases cognitive "reacting to."

Whether performers want to sustain or eliminate aesthetic distance during a performance, performers and audience must recognize that it is a fragile, delicate agreement. Its presence is needed for the aesthetic experience of the performing arts to happen. It operates with the willing suspension of disbelief to create the magic moments of performance.

Conclusion

The process of responding to the performing arts is complex. Our brains synthesize both the left-brain and right-brain stimuli. Simultaneously, we shift from the social experience of the performance to the aesthetic experience. We maintain the proper aesthetic distance in relation to the performance, while willingly suspending our disbelief to involve ourselves in the aesthetic experience. All this time we are actively "reacting with." Responding to the performing arts is an active rather than a passive experience. Active choices as audience members enhance our responses, and improves the quality of our experience with the performing arts.

CHAPTER 3

Enhancing Your Response to the Performing Arts

Audiences must actively listen. Active listening implies you are bringing an informed, inquisitive mind to a performance, and engaging your mind with the performance's visual, aural, and/or verbal stimuli. Active listening enhances your response to the performing arts. Several specific actions will improve your active listening in audiences.

Psychological and Physical Condition

We often attend the performing arts as an escape from a long day of work. Our minds, full of the day's problems, attempt to plan and organize tomorrow's solutions. Our bodies, fatigued from the rigors of 8 to 12 hours of activity, yearn for rest. Adding to these immediate difficulties, at dinner your date/spouse talks of family or relationship problems. You eat and drink too much at dinner as solace for your "sea" of troubles. And, when you finally get to the theatre, you realize that the play tonight is Shakespeare! Three hours of Shakespeare push your physical state and psychological feelings to an all-time low.

Active listening demands minds and bodies in proper condition for receiving performances. You cannot expect high returns on your performing arts investment, if your psychological and physical "stake" is low. What actions can you take to improve your condition to receive a performance?

Ideally the more rested your mind and body, the more receptive they will be for active listening. However, more often than not, the ideal conditions do not exist. Even under the worst conditions, the following suggestions may help prepare you psychologically and physically for performances.

1. Find your method of mentally and physically disposing of the day's tensions and problems before the performance. For some people exercise helps: jogging, walking, tennis, handball, swimming, aerobics. Physical activity rejuvenates the mind and body. Other people prefer a long, leisurely dinner, or other activity that allows you to unwind. Whatever your choice, avoid activities/discussions which will increase tension or keep your mind preoccupied with daily worries.
2. Use the time before a performance to anticipate the play, ballet, or concert. Over dinner or on the way to a Shakespearean play, review the plot; share other Shakespeare plays or productions; talk about your usual difficulties with Shakespeare and how they might be surmounted. Not only will this discussion prepare you mentally for the performance, but also it fills your mind with thoughts other than business or personal problems.
3. Use your time in the theatre before the performance to prepare for the aesthetic experience. Read the program, especially notes, articles, or discussions which focus on the music, dance, play, composer, playwright, choreographer, musician, actor, or dancer featured in the performance. Look at the environment: the set on stage, or the musicians preparing. Listen to any pre-show music. Talk with your companion about the anticipated performance. Most important: give yourself 2–5 minutes of quiet time to relax and prepare for the performance.
4. Avoid letting your background fill your mind with negative thoughts before or during the performance. You focus your thoughts; you control what fills your mind. Fill your mind with thoughts which open, not close, your mind to the performance.
5. During the performance choose actions that utilize R-mode thinking, that encourage cognitive and emotional reacting with, and that focus on the aesthetic experience. You control to a great extent your reception of a performance.

If you practice these suggestions, you help yourself psychologically and physically in receiving any performance. When a performance is "working," you soon will be drawn into its magic. When a performance has aesthetic problems, you will be prepared to evaluate its weaknesses and to explore its strengths. The prepatory suggestions make you ready to actively respond.

Knowledge and Experience

Nothing enhances your responses to performing arts more quickly than acquiring knowledge about the arts and experience of performances. Any activity is more enjoyable when you have knowledge about it, and even more so when experience complements the knowledge. Maximum growth in your response to performances demands a commmitment to acquiring knowledge and experience.

Knowledge of the performing arts can be theoretical or practical. By reading, attending lectures, and/or taking courses you can gain detailed information about the history, the artistic and technical elements, the production practices, and performance literature of any performing art. Reading biographies and autobiographies introduces you to the lives of artists. Videos and television programs feature in depth examinations of the performing arts and their artists. Practical knowledge requires instruction and practice in acting, music, dance, or television/radio/film performance. Backstage work in the design and construction of sets, costumes, or lighting gives insights into the arts. Getting knowledge enhances the quality of your responses.

Attending performances increases your experience. The benefits of experience are attitudinal, i.e., your comfort and confidence at performances deepens, and incremental, i.e., your performance knowledge grows with each attendance. By combining knowledge and experience incredible intensifying of your understanding of performances occurs.

Listening to Enhance R-Mode Thinking

Specific listening skills enhance R-mode thinking during performances. The "language" being used to communicate the art affects R-mode listening techniques. However, several generalized principles of enhancing right brain processing of the performing arts apply to all.

Enhancing R-mode processing in the performing arts begins with knowledge about the hemispherical differences of the brain. Awareness of how the right and left hemispheres process stimuli increases your potential to access R-mode thinking. This knowledge guides your holistic listening choices in performance situations.

To access R-mode audience members must choose specific actions while watching and listening to performances. Betty Edwards, author of *Drawing on the Right Brain* and *Drawing on the Artist Within,* asserts that to access the R-mode you must present L-mode with a task that it will reject. An example Edwards uses is turning a photograph upside-down and attempting to draw it. L-mode makes no sense of this assignment and rejects involvement. R-mode is then able to operate undisturbed. The success of this approach in drawing is fully illustrated Edwards' books.

In the performing arts dance and music especially provide examples of presenting L-mode with unacceptable tasks. At a dance performance you might focus on a dancer's body as it responds to the music and moves through space; on the spatial patterns created by several dancers; or on the emotional impact of the color and direction of the lighting in relation to the dance. At a music performance you might focus on listening to the various elements of music (melody, rhythm, tone color, form, or harmony); on the physical actions of a performer; or on the visual aspects of the performance environment.

Finding a rejectable task for L-mode in theatre, film, or television performance is more difficult. Because dramatic performance is verbal, L-mode is always engaged. However, even during verbal moments of a production, you can choose tasks that L-mode will reject. And, during moments of silence and pure action, the performance may bombard R-mode with visual and aural sensations. The spatial aspects of the performance stimulates R-mode: the set design and furniture arrangement, the visual dazzle of special effects, and the actors as objects in space as they move from composition to composition. Also, awareness of color is a R-mode task. The colors in the set, costumes, and lighting and their effect on your perceptions are not particularly interesting to L-mode. Finally, the actors' nonverbal action stimulates the brain's right hemisphere.

Another approach that enhances right brain involvement is simply letting the performance happen: as you receive the varied stimuli just accept the sensations. Consciously choose not to let the left brain evaluate, analyze, make sense, or give order to the stimuli. Like a gentle ocean wave washing over your body on a warm summer day at the beach, allow the performing arts experience to wash over you. All the stimuli will be received. Some will be immediately understood and related to; others will be puzzling, unfamiliar, and unknown. Avoid *at the moment of experience* any attempts at judging, rationalizing, or making sense of the experience. By avoiding these activities, your right brain has maximal input into the process of dealing with all the information received from the performance.

After the performance you will have a response. Some responses will be expressed immediately; other responses will take longer, especially if you are puzzled and confused. The mind, which dislikes the chaotic and disordered, will bring order to and make sense of these other responses. *After* the performance is the time for the left brain to use its powers in relation to the stimuli the whole brain has already received and processed.

Your responses to a performance function as criticism. As your ability to receive and process the whole performance grows, your criticism of the performing arts will improve. Expanding your right hemisphere capabilities will not only increase your enjoyment of the performing arts, but also in the end make your L-mode thinking about them, i.e., your criticism, more informed and perceptive.

A final comment about left brain, right brain functions. Our brain integrates all of our experiences. Even though research validates the hemispheric division of the brain, the interaction between the hemispheres is cooperative and complementary. Each hemisphere influences what we think and how we deal with information. We can never shut off completely one side or the other. However, we can provide experiences and stimuli for either side to process. The performing arts will definitely stimulate your right hemisphere.

The Aftermath and Its Importance

What happens after a performance is the aftermath. The aftermath can be as insignificant or as significant as you wish to make it. It breaks down into two parts: 1) the group experience occuring immediately after the performance ends, and 2) the individual response occuring after the audience leaves the theatre.

Typically the audience as a group applauds the performers' efforts. For a brief moment this applause, the "curtain call" integrates the social and aesthetic experiences of the performance. The curtain call recognizes the aesthetic achievement of the performers in the social context; it is the audience's way to immediately respond to the artist.

However, the group response primarily serves as our re-entry into the social realm. With the end of the applause and raising of the auditiorium lights, the re-emergence of the social awareness of the performance encourages our individual responses. We may exchange comments of satisfaction with other audience members. We may immediately share comments of pleasure or scorn with our companions. The aftermath's real importance occurs in your considered private responses expressed to others or to yourself.

Putting into words what you feel is difficult. Putting into words your perceptions of a performance is difficult. However, this process of expressing ideas and emotions through words is a necessary and important part of the aftermath. Verbalizing your reactions brings the performance process to its closure. Using our previous knowledge and experience, the aftermath serves as an opportunity for analysis and synthesis of our perceptions. The performance, which began as a social experience, has its aesthetic elements understood in the social experience of the aftermath.

"What to say" about theatre, dance, music, film, and television/radio is addressed in the subsequent chapters. "Critical perspectives" about the performing arts are looked at in the chapter on criticism. Needless to say, your continued study and experiencing of the performing arts will expand your potentials and abilities to verbalize your ideas and feelings.

PART II

The Performing Arts

You should have a better understanding how audiences function as part of the performing arts experience. What you bring and how you respond are crucial parts of any performance. The audience is the important final link—the receiver—in the performing arts communication model.

Just as important as the receiver in the performing arts communication model is the source of the stimuli being communicated—the individual performing art. Certain generalizations about how the arts communicate apply to all the performing arts. However, each art has a "language" of its own, i.e., a special means of communicating to an audience. Knowing how each art works its magic enhances your appreciation of the art and increases your enjoyment of a performance.

The goal of the second part of this book is to provide you with the needed knowledge about each of the performing arts. This knowledge consists of the basic information, the special "language" of each art, which will allow your mind access to the performance. Knowing as much as possible about each performance fulfills part of your responsibility as a good audience member. This knowledge should complement and interact with what you know about how audiences work.

Each of the performing arts is complex. Each has a rich history, a wide and varied performance literature, various performance styles, and a complicated training in the techniques of performance. No one book could do justice to an in-depth study of each art.

Our study will focus on a basic question: what information does a general audience member need to understand and enjoy a performance? The answers to this question presume that, if one of the arts is particularly interesting, you can explore it in more detail. The bibliography at the end of the book suggests sources for further study of each art.

CHAPTER 4

Theatre

What Is Theatre?

Everyday we probably experience a performance of drama. If you watch one hour of television each day, you probably see a soap opera, a dramatic series, or a comedy series. Although these are drama performances they are not "theatre." If you attend the movies, you may see adventure, comic, or serious dramatic films. These are not "theatre."

Theatre is a performing art with definite component parts. A simple definition might be: theatre is a live performance of a drama by actors before an audience. We will discover that theatre is more complex than this, but this definition emphasizes its important elements.

Theatre is a "live" performance "before an audience." This distinguishes it from film and television, which are recorded arts, i.e., recorded before they are actually shown to an audience. Theatre happens at the same time the audience receives the performance. As a temporal art, theatre exists only at the time it is happening. Without the audience the performance does not exist; it is merely another rehearsal. The theatre performance and the audience exist in the same time frame and in the same space, the theatre building.

The Theatre Performance and Communication

The theatre performance uses some basic elements: drama, actors, design, and direction. Although theatre may exist with only actors playing on a bare stage before an audience, our

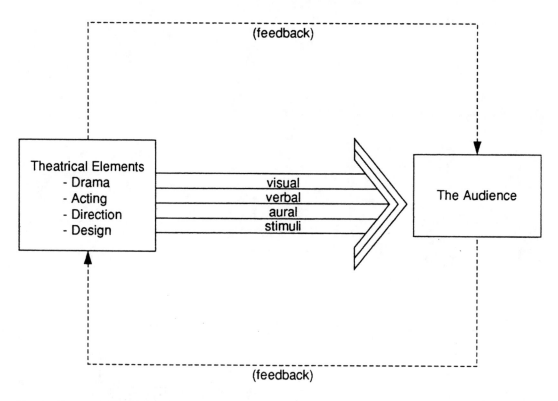

(feedback)

Theatrical Elements
- Drama
- Acting
- Direction
- Design

visual
verbal
aural
stimuli

The Audience

(feedback)

Theatre Communication Model.

usual experience incorporates the four basic elements mentioned above. How these elements interact can be understood by examining the Theatre Communication Model.

Like any performing art, theatre's primary purpose is communication. Theatre explores the major issues of human existence by revealing them in the emotional and intellectual relationships of characters involved in dramatic action. The interactions can be comic or serious. Through observation the audience learns about the condition of being human. What is being communicated, the content of the message, is found in the script being performed: the drama. The playwright has created and fixed in time the dramatic action, characters, and dialogue. Theatre artists interpret this text and communicate it using the special "language" of theatrical art.

Theatre utilizes all the potential stimuli that audiences may receive—verbal, aural, and visual. Theatre artists shape their art to communicate the overall idea of the drama. The actor creates using not only the verbal—the words of the playwright—but also colors them through the use of voice, gesture, and movement; acting stimulates both left and right brain for the audience. The design elements of scenery, costume, lighting, and makeup employ the visual exclusively; the design of elements of music and sound appeal aurally. Design stimulates the right brain for the audience.

Although audiences notice and remember the crafts of the playwright and actor, the most influential artist in today's theatre is the director. The director unifies and coordinates the acting and design elements in order to communicate the drama's meaning to the audience. The ultimate responsibility for the success or failure of a performance is the director's.

The final link in the Theatre Communication Model is the audience. Without the audience there is no communication, because without a receiver true communication does not exist. If the communication is organized, coordinated, and planned, the audience receives the message the theatre artists intended. Poor theatre happens when theatre artists do not shape their artistic processes and send disorganized and chaotic messages to audiences.

Special Qualities of Theatre

When audiences leave theatrical performances they are probably talking about the drama and/or the actors. This is not unusual. In the 4th century B.C., the Greek philosopher, Aristotle, defined ''mimesis'' —the imitation of action—as the crucial reason why people like dramatic art. We enjoy watching other people and their behaviors. Theatre resembles life more than any performing art. For this reason alone we would find it compelling.

Lifelikeness is a unique quality of theatre. The subject of theatre, expressed in the drama, is human experience and action. Theatre uses live human beings interacting before us; actors bring to life the actions and experiences of the play's characters. No wonder these theatrical components draw the audience's first reactions.

Another special quality of theatre is its ephemeral nature. Being *ephemeral* means that the theatre experience is short-lived; it exists in time for split seconds and then disappears and becomes part of the past. And, as part of the past, it is not reclaimable. Theatre is a temporal art; it is not fixed-in-time.

Like other performing arts theatre is also *most objective*. We discover information about the characters and the action through objective observation. What characters say and do gives us information about their internal and external qualities. No other source for the information intervenes. The playwright, unlike the novelist, comments on the character's behavior only through dramatic action and dialogue.

Theatre is a *complex* art. Different artists collaborate to create a theatrical performance. The playwright is a literary artist. The actors are performance artists. Scenic, costume, and lighting designers and technicians realize the visual arts in a production. Musicians and sound designers add their special skills. And, finally the director coordinates all their work, plus adding the contributions of the director's art—development of production concept, guiding actors, composition and movement. Many individual arts comprise the production.

Theatre's most special quality is its *immediacy*. The experience of theatre involves live actors who are immediately interacting with a live audience in the same environment and at the same time. The electricity of this relationship makes theatre a very personal art.

Theatre's ephemeral, objective, complex, and immediate natures increase its lifelike qualities. Life possesses all these qualities. It is ephemeral, experienced in short-lived episodes which become immediately part of the past. Life is objective: we learn about ourselves and other people only through observation and experience. It is complex and immediate, being composed of thousands upon thousands of events which fill our present moments. The fact that theatre's special qualities relate to its lifelikeness only reinforces that magical power theatre art exerts over us.

Types of Theatre: Representational and Presentational

Two types of theatre exist for audiences: representational and presentational. Since most of us are more experienced with the representational style from film and TV, we often make assumptions about theatre performances based on our representational experiences. Understanding the components of both types of theatre will increase your potential enjoyment of both. Also, since much theatre today combines both presentational and representational, understanding these terms may lessen confusion during the theatre experience.

Representational Theatre

Representational theatre is illusory theatre. The theatre artists make an effort to convince the audience that a stage is not a stage, and that actors are not really actors. Actors use all their skills to appear like "real" people. Communication between the actors and the audience is indirect, i.e., actors only talk to other actors onstage and never speak directly to the audience. The stage itself is an area of illusion: design elements disguise the stage as if it were a "real" place, e.g., rooms are designed, decorated, and lighted as if they were authentic living spaces for people.

In representational theatre the audience becomes the place of actuality, and the stage area the place of illusion. This is achieved by creating a sense of distance, or spatial discontinuity, between the audience and the stage. Various technical devices create this sense of spatial discontinuity: the use of a stage curtain separates the stage and the audience, and the house lights are lowered so that the stage remains in light while the audience sits in a darkened space.

Examples of representational theatre are numerous. In theatre history the theatre of 3rd-4th century Greece, the European medieval mystery plays, and the theatres of Antoine in France in the late 19th century and Belasco in the United States in the early 20th century were representational to a significant degree. Much of our theatre today remains repre-

Representational theatre elements are captured in the design elements for the Guthrie Theater's 1981 production of FOXFIRE, by Susan Cooper and Hume Cronyn, directed by Marshall W. Mason, with Jessica Tandy as Annie Nations, William Newman as Prinz Carpenter. (Courtesy of The Guthrie Theater. Photograph by Bruce Goldstein.)

sentational, especially drama on television and in film. The "soap opera" is a daily testament to the power of the representational theatre.

Presentational Theatre

Presentational theatre is non-illusory theatre. Actors do not lose their identities as actors. The audience does not regard them as a "real" person but as actors acting. Make-up, costume, movement, and speech emphasize the difference between the actor and a "real" person. In presentational theatre actors on occasion communicate directly with their audience.

The stage in presentational theatre is a platform for acting, not a disguised area. The design elements reinforce the concept that the stage is really a stage, a platform where actors perform and nothing more. Although the stage is distinguished from the rest of the theatre building, it is not presented as spatially discontinuous from it. Often with presenta-

Costumes and properties create the realism associated with representational theatre in the 1987 Shaw Festival production of MAJOR BARBARA by Bernard Shaw, directed by Christopher Newton, with Ted Dykstra as Snobby Price, Helen Taylor as Jenny Hill, and Martha Burns as Major Barbara Undershaft. (Courtesy of the Shaw Festival, Niagara-on-the-Lake, Ontario, Canada. Photograph by David Cook.)

tional theatre a stage curtain is not even used. In these situations actors, audience, and performance exist within the same psychologically undifferentiated world.

Theatre, past and present, give us many examples of presentational theatre. Oriental theatre, 5th century Greek theatre, the public playhouses of Shakespeare's time, and American vaudeville performances are historical examples of this type. Today we see presentational theatre everytime we attend our favorite musical or opera, experience any contemporary experimental theatre, or watch improvisational comedy like *Monty Python* or *Saturday Night Live.*

The distinctions between these two kinds of theatre blur when audiences confront contemporary dramatic presentations in the theatre, in film, or on television. Contemporary playwrights and theatre artists often use both types of theatre within one performance. In plays that are primarily representational, playwrights have characters communicate directly

The non-illusory qualities of presentational theatre are highlighted in The Guthrie Theater's 1983 production of the musical GUYS AND DOLLS, staged by Garland Wright and featuring Roy Thinnes as Sky Masterson. (Courtesy of The Guthrie Theater, Minneaspolis, MN. Photograph by Joe Giannetti.)

with the audience. Directors have actors perform scenes in the auditorium breaking spatial discontinuity. Set designers dispense with the stage curtain and allow the audience immediate viewing of a representational set. In film and television characters in representational drama will address audience members directly to make comments on the dramatic action.

What does this artistic flexibility to utilize both types of theatre mean for the audience? Audiences must remain open to receiving theatre communication in both representational and presentational modes in the same production. Experiencing a wide variety of theatre will give you the flexibility to shift your methods of perceiving the theatre performance. Your flexibility to adjust between representational and presentational will allow you to go with whatever style the theatre artist throws at you. This ability will increase your enjoyment of theatre.

The "Language" of Theatre

To enjoy theatre you must understand its "language," i.e., how theatre artists communicate. The theatre performance conveys the emotions and ideas of human interaction to the audience through the work of playwrights, actors, directors, and designers. These artists "talk" to you in different ways, using methods and practices specific to their arts and crafts.

We are going to explore the individual theatre artist's language. Each component part of theatre will be studied from the perspective of how the artist communicates and of what knowledge the audience needs of each art to enjoy fully the theatre experience. Each component deserves more discussion than the objectives for this book permit. Therefore, a bibliography of additional reading in all the areas of theatre is provided at the end of the chapter. Also, since many of the theatrical components apply to the "language" used in the other performing arts, the material of this chapter will be referred to in later chapters.

Drama

The "fixed" element of theatre is the drama. Written prior to the process of theatrical production, it remains after a production has ended. Drama communicates verbally; ideas, emotion, action are all communicated through language. Its verbal nature allows it to be fixed-in-time as a literary art.

Drama as a literary art is much different from other forms, like the novel or poetry. Drama is written with the expressed purpose of being performed by actors before an audience. Although we may read drama, we must realize that the playwright intended his work to be communicated through the theatrical elements.

The drama has a powerful impact on the audience, because it is the imitation of human action. Aristotle, the 4th century B.C. Greek philosopher, in *The Poetics* had labeled this particular quality as "mimesis."

> . . . The instinct of imitation is implanted in man from childhood . . . and through imitation learns his earliest lessons; and it is also natural to delight in imitations. We have evidence of this in the facts of experience. Objects which in themselves we view with pain, we delight to contemplate when reproduced with minute fidelity . . . The cause of this again is that to learn gives the liveliest pleasure, not only to philosophers, but to men in general . . . Thus the reason why men enjoy seeing a likeness is that in contemplating it they find themselves learning of inferring, and saying perhaps, "Ah, that is he."[1]

---

1. S.H. Butcher, *Aristotle's Theory of Poetry and Fine Art.* London: Macmillan, 1907. p. 15.

However, unlike the random and unpredictable nature of life, drama is a controlled, selective ordering of human experience. The selection and ordering of the imitation of human action found in any drama is the creative activity of the playwright. Understanding the basic components of a play will clarify the playwright's creative contribution to a theatrical performance.

Components of Drama

Aristotle in *The Poetics* defined the six elements of drama and ranked them in the order of their importance: plot, characters, theme, diction, music, and spectacle. These elements and their ordering still define the major components of drama, and their importance for audiences.

Plot is the story of the play, or simply what happens in the drama. The characters of the drama tell the story through "dramatic action." Plot depends on action to sustain audience interest. Without effective dramatic action a play is boring for an audience. The plot has its own structure:

1. *Exposition.* This beginning phase of the plot introduces you to the characters, the dramatic action, and the environment of the play. We must learn everything through characters talking to one another; dialogue contains all the dramatic action of the play. Without a doubt the exposition is the least interesting part of the drama for the audience. At this point you know nothing about the characters or the dramatic action, and have little involvement with the drama.

2. *Conflict.* All effective drama has conflict, i.e., strongly opposing forces within the dramatic action. In drama these forces are usually embodied in different characters who represent different points of view. The results of the conflict may be comic, like Felix vs. Oscar in *The Odd Couple,* or tragic, like Willy Loman vs. his son Biff in *The Death of a Salesman.* The major conflicts in a drama are introduced in the exposition and revealed in the complications.

3. *Complications.* To make the plot interesting and to reveal the conflict, the playwright introduces complications to the story. The complications increase the tension of the conflict, and build to the climax of the play.

4. *Climax.* The point of highest interest in the plot of a drama is the climax. This point usually occurs after a build in complications. From this point the clash of forces has changed the characters; they are not the same as they at the beginning of the play.

5. *Denouement.* The last portion of the plot is the unraveling, solution, or clarification provided in the denouement. Occurring after the climax, it can consist of several pages or a single line. The denouement brings the plot to its final resolution and outcome.

Characters are the means the playwright must use to reveal the dramatic action, or plot of a drama. Drama as a form allows for no descriptions of action or authorial revelation of a character's thoughts as a novel or short story does. What is revealed about the characters and the dramatic action comes from three sources:

1. What characters say.
2. What characters do, i.e., what their actions reveal.
3. What other characters say about them.

The characters in a play evolve through their verbal and physical actions. Therefore, playwrights must create credible characters, whose actions are believable for audiences. Clearly we must be able to see what a character wants (objective), what is preventing the character from getting that desire (obstacle), and what ways the character is taking to get around the obstacle (action). Certainly the more that characters are like us, the more able we are to identify with them; empathy increases. However, because of "mimesis," any human activity and behavior has the potential of involving us emotionally or cognitively. The universal nature of human behavior is a powerful force.

The *theme* of the drama is the major idea or the message of the drama. Some plays have a simple, single message. For example, using a filmed drama that we all know, the theme of the classic film *The Wizard of Oz* might be stated as "There's no place like home." The plot and characters of Oz reinforce this central idea. However, some plays may explore a variety of themes: *King Lear* focuses on several including the relationships of parent to children, the nature of power, and the meaning of love. In a good play the theme reveals itself through plot and characters. The plot's dramatic action as embodied in the characters leads the audience to the major idea.

Diction is the choice of words the playwright uses to carry the dramatic action of the plot, to evolve characters through action, and to reveal the theme. The playwright depends on words to tell the story. However, the words must fit each character. Romeo's response at seeing his love Juliet in the orchard appropriately captures the quality and nature of this particular young romantic:

> It is my lady! O it is my love!
> O that she knew she were!
> She speaks yet she says nothing, what of that?
> Her eye discourses, I will answer it.
> I am too bold, 'tis not to me she speaks.
> Two of the fairest stars in all the heaven,
> Having some business, do entreat her eyes
> To twinkle in their spheres till they return.
> (II,i,52–59)

However, these words would seem laughable coming from the mouth of a teenager today. Diction must propel the plot, but also artfully create unique and credible characters for the audience. The use of profanity on stage and in film arises from playwright's trying to cap-

The Guthrie Theater's productions of ST. JOAN by Bernard Shaw, and FRANKENSTEIN by Barbara Field illustrate Aristotle's concept of "spectacle." (Courtesy of The Guthrie Theater, Minneapolis, MN. Photographs by Joe Giannetti.)

ture the reality of contemporary behavior in drama. As our society has become less polite and formal, so has the language used in plays.

Music, more important in the drama of ancient Greece than in today's stage plays, sets moods for the audience. A director often chooses appropriate music to prepare the audience before the production, or to reinforce the action during the play. In today's theatre music also includes any use of sound effects, i.e., sounds which create a sense of place or imagined action, in today's theatre. Finally, certain types of theatre have developed which depend on music for their impact, e.g., opera and musical theatre. The almost constant music score found in most contemporary film testifies to its emotional impact.

Spectacle includes all the visual elements of theatre. Although these visual effects are important parts of the design element of theatre, they rank last in Aristotle's list. Spectacle supports the essential dramatic action of the plot, the characters, and the theme of the play. However, Aristotle felt that the essence of drama is plot and characters.

Acting

What do audiences talk about as they leave a theatrical performance? If you are like most people, you and your friends are talking about the play, i.e., the dramatic action, and the actors, i.e., the theatre artists who embody the characters. Although the setting and costumes may have been wonderful, the lighting superb, and the directing first-rate, your first attention is focused on the actors and the play. Our delight in mimesis, i.e., the imitation of action, makes plot and characters particularly memorable components of drama in performance.

The theatrical element most involved with plot and characters are the actors. Through their art and skill actors "flesh out" the characters' personalities and traits, and drive the action of the plot to its climax. It is no surprise that audiences single out actors for comment after a production.

Not only is acting the most compelling theatrical element, but it also helps the theatre serve as an excellent source of information about people. Actors bring fictional characters to life just as if they were living before our eyes. Through the theatre we may catch a glimpse of historical periods and people that previously have only existed for us in history books. Through the theatre and the work of actors, we may meet types of people unknown to us in our daily lives. People from different social classes, vocations, ethnic groups, and psychological orientations live and breathe before our eyes. For the "two hours traffic of the stage" we experience their lives, their thoughts, and their feelings. We gain a better understanding of how other people think and feel. Theatre introduces us to the variety of humankind through the art of acting, which brings the drama to life.

Audiences appreciate acting for a reason unrelated to the drama itself. As an art acting is immediately understood, almost without any formal knowledge of its nature. In contrast with other performing artists, e.g., musicians and dancers, whose artistic skills and proficiencies may overwhelm audiences, actors practice the most accessible of all the arts.

Excellent acting appears so natural, merely a slight extension of everyday conversation. Audience members may think and sometimes say:

> " I could act, if I wanted to. What's so special about acting? Memorize some lines and talk. I talk everyday. Anybody can act.''

No one would think, let alone speak, those same words about a ballet dancer or a violinist, whose performance skills and techniques are so obviously difficult to master. In contrast acting seems like taking everyday interactions and putting them on stage or screen. In fact we know we ''act'' everyday in our lives, giving little performances to impress or amuse our friends and coworkers. We may feel that acting on stage must not be that different.

Acting's accessibility as an art allows for our immediate appreciation. However, accessibility also leads to confusing ''roleplaying'' or ''role presentation'' in life with acting on stage. Clarification of these concepts will distinguish their similarities and differences.

What Is Roleplaying or Role Presentation?

Every human being actively roleplays everyday. The average person plays 25 different roles in a lifetime. As you interact with your family, friends, teachers, employers, and business people, you are roleplaying. Roleplaying is a unified pattern of behavior revealing part of an individual's total nature. Role presentation may really be a more accurate term, since roleplaying suggests that we may be consciously pretending to be something or someone other than our ''real'' self. Role presentation implies that we will always present *part* of our total self in our interactions with people.

Our personality could be seen as a complex structure consisting of an ''I'' and several ''me's''. The ''I'' is our sense of identity. The various ''me's'' can be radically different parts of our identity. You can think of yourself, your identity, your ''I'' as an apple, and the various ''me's'' as slices of that apple. Just as one slice of the apple does not represent the whole apple, so no one ''me'' (or role) represents your total identity (or ''self'') .

You are most aware of the conflicts between the roles you present whenever you must present two different roles at the same time. Think of your inner conflict as a teenager when you invited friends to your home and your parents wanted to sit in the living room talking to them, or when you and your date met a teacher at a drive-in movie, or when your little brother stayed when you and a date wanted to be alone.

Role presentation is a natural human behavior; we adapt our behavior to our circumstances and present an aspect of ourselves, our personalities, to others. This behavior can be conscious, i.e., we are aware that we are modifying our behavior, or unconscious, i.e., we are unaware that we are modifying our behavior. During a job interview, we are consciously aware of our role presentation behavior; we are creating the most positive image of ourselves for a prospective employer. When we talk to our mothers and fathers, we are usually unaware of the modifications in our behavior to adapt to the personalities of our parents; we will be subtly or unsubtly a different son/daughter to our mothers than to our fathers.

Why do people roleplay? All role presentations relate to creating positive impressions on other people, and to creating an acceptable "self." Roleplaying allows us to control the responses of others toward us and to pursue the basic goals all humans want—prestige, respect, affection, and power. Erving Goffman in *Role Presentation in Everyday Life* discusses the basic purposes of human roleplaying. It is in our interests to control the conduct of others, especially their responses toward us. When you appear in the presence of others, there will be some reason to mobilize your activity so that it convey an impression to others which it is in your interest to convey.

All humans roleplay. All roleplaying, either conscious or unconscious, is dependent on the situation and circumstances; outside forces may intervene; it is always spontaneous and improvised. Role presentation is part of the dynamic fabric of our daily existence.

What Is Acting?

You might ask: "Well . . . Isn't roleplaying in life just acting?" Although we will discover similarities between them, the art of acting and role presentation are not the same. The art of acting might be defined as conscious creative activity in which a performer using his/her voice, body, and emotion/mind simulates the behavior of a fictitious character.

The differences between acting and role presentation are significant.

Acting	Role Presentation
Acting is always conscious; actors always know that they are on stage performing.	Role presentation may be unconscious, i.e., we may present an aspect of ourselves without consciously controlling our behavior.
In acting a written script influences behavior.	In role presentation the circumstances of the situation influence our behavior.
In acting minimal outside forces interfere to modify the results of the script.	In role presentation outside forces often intervene to modify the results of the human interaction.
Little improvisation occurs during the traditional acting performance.	Improvisation is constantly occurring during the role presentation.

[Improvisation is the creation of dialogue and/or action at the moment of performance.]

Acting	Role Presentation
Acting is larger than life, i.e., the actor is modifying the performance to work in the theatre/film/television environment, and the changes are rehearsed and planned before the presentation occurs.	Role presentation is life.

Acting is significantly different from role presentation. Why then are they often confused? Why do some people feel that acting as an art is "no big thing" since they do it everyday?

Similarities between acting and *conscious* role presentation exist. The basic intent of both acting and conscious role presentation is the same—communication. Both characters in drama and people in real life use specific words and actions to communicate thoughts and feelings, and to shape others' perceptions. As actors and people attempt to communicate, they make the communication truthful and believable. The actor creates emotion to support a character's actions at a given point in a play; the student creates tears and feelings in order to convince a professor to change a grade. Believable communication of emotion and ideas are hallmarks of acting and *conscious* roleplaying.

The actor and the conscious roleplayer also use the same basic acting techniques. Actors learn in their training to focus their concentration and energy during a performance. Actors concentrate on the action of the moment, ignore distractions (like audience noises or camera movements), and keep their minds on their rehearsed choices for the character. This concentration and action—both mental and physical—demands energy to activate and sustain the character for the audience. Likewise the roleplayer—to create the desired presentation of self for a prospective employer, or a date, or a teacher—must concentrate on the present moment and energize and sustain mental and physical actions.

The actor and the conscious roleplayer also use their bodies and voices to create the presentation—either a character on stage or a conscious presentation of self to others. Actors may modify their bodies, faces, hairstyles, and voices to more appropriately embody a character from a play. Specific film actors' work come to mind as examples of this changeable nature of body and voice: Robert de Niro, Meryl Streep, and Dustin Hoffman are masters of the actor's art of physical and vocal transformation.

Although we may not resort to the extremes of actors, we modify ourselves physically and vocally when we consciously roleplay. It may only mean sitting more erect and controlling our hand gestures during an interview for a job. We might modify our hairstyles for a special date or party. We may change the way we walk or stand at a party. We may pitch our voices higher or lower in order to make them more attractive when meeting someone new. We may choose to maintain firm eye contact with our teachers and nod at appropriate times to suggest that we're listening and that we care about what we hear. The ways we use our bodies and voices as *conscious* roleplayers are similar to the ways actors use theirs on stage or in film.

By understanding these similarities and differences between acting and role presentation, the actor's art becomes an aesthetic activity differentiated from our daily roleplaying behavior. How actors create their art is the next step in increasing your understanding of this element of theatre.

The Psychology of Acting

Actors choose the art of acting for a lot of reasons. Like many careers, acting is a means to assert one's identity, one's sense of self. We gravitate towards careers which allow us to do this. Actors are unique, however, in that they communicate their experiences and emotions, and make themselves heard and seen *by simulating fictitious characters*. Most of us do not feel the need to memorize lines, rehearse appropriate emotions and actions for a character, and present this fictitious person before an audience. Why do actors need to express themselves in this unique manner?

Actors take a joy in "playing," an activity which demands transforming the unknown to the known, the mundane to the special, and the unreal to the real. We all remember our own childhood "play." Children, using creative imaginations and abilities to concentrate, turn everyday objects into space ships, doctors' offices, classrooms, and war zones, and themselves into space warriors, doctors, patients, teachers, parents, and soldiers. Most of us leave behind this imaginative play as we move into adolescence and adulthood; the ways of the world demand "work" not "play." Actors, on the other hand, expand these childhood games into their art. The abilities of concentration and creative imagination are used daily as actors "play" in their art. This childlike joy in playing is a crucial element of why actors choose to perform.

CALVIN & HOBBES at "play"—an important quality for all actors. (*Calvin & Hobbes* copyright 1987 Universal Press Syndicate. Reprinted with permission. All rights reserved.)

The joy of playing is only one childlike quality actors possess. Actors need to claim and maintain a childlike center of attention from others. As we came to perceive the world as infants, it seemed to revolve around us: when we cried parents rushed to our cribs; when we smiled, people hugged and kissed us; when we were hungry, Mother and Dad fed us. As we grew older, we discovered the worlds outside of ourselves: other brothers/sisters in our families; other children in the neighborhood and in schools; parents' other concerns. We had to adjust our need to maintain the center of attention; we had to find acceptable ways to gain approval. Actors' needs to claim the center of attention have the childlike quality of "look at me." This particular need develops in actors a strong, ego-centered personality.

A strong, ego-centered personality assures survival in the world of theatre, film, and television. Studies have shown that successful actors, i.e., those who have worked regularly in performance and earned their livings through acting, have a strong sense of self identity. This strong sense of self protects actors from the constant rejection actors face daily as they audition for roles. To be a "survivor" in the business of acting demands a strong, ego-centered personality. People often think that actors have turned to acting to compensate for strong inferiority complexes and to escape from their lives. Some may have, but they seldom achieve enduring success. Actors use their need to maintain that childlike center of attention to develop a sense of self-identity which will allow them to survive and persevere in the "dog-eat-dog" world of theatre/film/television.

A final need of actors which propels them toward a career in acting relates to the human need for approval, acceptance, and affection. We all possess this need to some degree. Most of us fulfill it through our families, friends, and relationships with another person. We have a relatively small circle of people who give us these needed "strokes." Actors possess the need for *mass* approval, acceptance, and affection; they need to know that hundreds, thousands, or even millions of people accept and love them. This strong need keeps them going during the hard times and sustains them during the good times. A simple manifestation of this need is the applause audiences give performers. Applause is our way to say—"Wonderful performance" or "I loved it" or "I love you!". The applause and cheering that often accompany the end of a performance is a powerful aphrodisiac that stimulates the actor to continue.

Actors choose acting for powerful psychological reasons. These reasons relate to fulfilling themselves artistically, emotionally, and intellectually. These psychological reasons can influence choices, and make some people more susceptible to the lures of a career in acting. However, a psychological predisposition for acting alone does not assure someone success. Acting is an art, which demands rigorous training. Exploring the elements of this training will increase your appreciation for the art of acting.

Training and the Art of Acting

Actor training works toward the development of *technique*. Technique depends on the viewpoints that are received during training. Some training emphasizes the internal, emotional aspects of performance; others emphasize the external, physical aspects of performance. The ideal training program presents a balance, since the actor uses both internal and external elements. An inclusive definition of technique is acting skills that can be repeated on demand.

This practical definition of technique focuses on the three components of acting— voice, body, and mind—which are the "colors" actors use to create their art. Just as painters place different colors on their palettes to use and combine on their canvases, so actors use and combine their voices, bodies, and minds to bring characters to life in the theatre. What audiences see and hear is the result of actors' technique developed through training.

An actor's voice conveys the meaning of the playwright's dialogue to the audience. Audiences must understand and feel the meaning of the words. To communicate both understanding and feeling demands a flexible vocal instrument, one that the actor can control to achieve the desired results. Actors train the vocal instrument daily through various exercises that work to increase vocal strength and projection, to modify the voice's quality, to expand vocal range and variety, and to make the articulation of sounds precise and accurate. These vocal exercises remain a part of the actors' repertory of daily training activities throughout their career.

Actors need bodily self-awareness and control. Not only must actors recognize and control personal physical mannerisms that may distract, but also they must feel comfortable with and control their bodies in space. The space referred to is the three dimensional cube of the acting area. With every movement an actor communicates a message to the audience. Whether the movement is walking across the space, or picking up a teacup, or striking another character to the floor with a fist, it must communicate the appropriate message. The message may be an aspect of a character's personality, or age, or temperament; it may communicate a character's specific want or objective; or it may capture the emotion of a given moment onstage. Dance training, fencing, yoga, tai-chi, and/or stage combat may lead actors to bodily self-awareness and control. These training methods are not an end in themselves, but increase the actor's awareness and control over the body in space.

For audiences voice and body are the most apparent components of the actor's art. Training can most visibly affect these components. They are often referred to as the "technical" elements of acting, in the sense that specific exercises and practices may cause growth in ability and skill. The component least visible and technical is the actor's mind.

Just as audience members use their right and left hemispheres to respond to a performance, actors involve their whole brains in bringing their art to life. In rehearsal and performance the actor's mind is engaged in revealing the character's world.

Rehearsal thinking for actors involves both the analytical left and the visual/emotional right brains. Actors spend much time in analyzing the script to discover what their characters are like. They must understand the characters' objectives, emotions, physical characteristics, and relationships; the source of this detailed information is the script. The play may take place in a different time, or an unknown locale, or may involve unique groups, e.g., salesmen or Viet Nam veterans. Then, actors must research specifically the history, customs, environment, and psychological/sociological backgrounds of periods, locales, or groups by using sources other than the script.

In the rehearsal process the actors organize their behaviors and actions for the eventual performance. They memorize lines in a specific order; they coordinate their lines with the movements for the character as defined by the director and with the gestures appropriate for the character; and they coordinate their actions and lines with all the other characters who interact with them during the play. Finally, in rehearsal actors evaluate their work and with the help of the director grow and develop in their characters using their acting skills. All of this rehearsal behavior demands actively involving the left hemisphere of the brain.

Actors have very dominant right brains. They need the right brain to succeed in their art. Some right brain skills may have been developing since childhood. Acting training perfects them. Without these abilities an actor's performance may possess technical mastery, but will not engage the audience's emotions.

Imagination, a quality all of us have to some degree, is a most important right brain attribute for actors. Imagination is the ability to form mental images of things that are not actually present; it is the ability of the right hemisphere to visualize. Creative people from artists to writers to scientists possess active imaginations; so do actors.

Actors use their imaginations in a special way. They indulge in creative fantasy, an active form of imagining. Actors give the appearance of reality to events which may not happened to them. No matter how close the life of a character may be to the actual events in an actor's life, it is rarely exactly the same. Therefore, actors must use their imaginations through creative fantasy to transform themselves into the reality of the character and the play. Actors face these creative transformations daily as they play beggars or kings, drug king-pins or stock brokers, and as they explore actions onstage as extreme as dying. Imagination and creative fantasy, important elements of an actor's art, need constant nurturing through training and performance.

Creative fantasy for actors also involves emotional transformations, i.e., drawing upon the emotional experiences and observations of the actors' lives to reveal the emotions and feelings of the characters. Emotional transformation is the actor's most powerful tool. To transform personal emotions into character emotions actors must be able to feel strongly their and others' emotions, and be able to express those emotions onstage. As part of acting training, exercises and games help actors release emotions. However, unlike exercises to train voice and body, they will not absolutely assure growth and development. An actor's individual concept of self determines how easily and comfortably emotions will be revealed publicly. Actors essentially do private things in public. These highly emotional actions demand a richly imaginative and accessible right hemisphere of the brain.

The ability to concentrate is a crucial skill for the actor. Concentration is simply the ability to focus all one's attention on the present moment. For a character to be alive for an audience, an actor must be bringing it to life in the present. To do this an actor's thoughts, actions, and emotions must be actively immersed in the present moment. This simple task is really quite difficult.

Test your ability at concentration. Try to keep your thoughts concerned only with your present circumstances. Try to sustain your concentration on the present moment as long as you can. If your mind starts to evaluate, to wonder why you are doing this, to slip into the future, or to wander to past events, renew your concentration on the present moment.

Did you discover what helped you to stay in the present moment? The real key to increasing our powers of concentration is to heighten our awareness of the input of the senses—sight, hearing, touch, taste, and smell. If we fill our minds with thoughts stimulated by our senses, we keep ourselves in the present moment. If you are thinking about what you are seeing, hearing, touching, tasting, or smelling, you are alive in the present moment. The same rules apply when you are interacting with someone. By giving over your focus to the individual, i.e., what they are saying, how they look, etc., your concentration does not wander. Concentration is easiest when we are talking, because our minds are filled with thoughts and our attempts to express them. For this reason, actors usually find it easy to concentrate when they have lines to speak.

Skills in concentration can grow. Through the process of exercises, games, scene work, and play rehearsal, actors expand their present limits of concentration to the level needed for successful performance. Besides keeping themselves actively in the present moment, actors also must concentrate on all the elements of technique, characterization, and performance. Concentration, a complex task combining both right and left brain functions, is essential for excellent acting.

Actors are their own instruments. To play their instruments well demands rigorous training, so that all elements of technique—voice, body, and mind—are ready for performance. When all the elements of technique are operating at their optimum levels, an actor is ready to move an audience to realms of experience and emotion that it has not imagined.

Design

Design is the visual/aural scheme of the production, including scenery, costumes, properties, lighting, music/sound, and makeup. These visual/aural elements help to communicate the director's concept and playwright's ideas. Therefore, the function or purpose of design is to assist the audience's perception of the production by stimulating emotional or cognitive responses. The language of design is visual or aural, and appeals primarily to the right hemisphere of the brain. Increasing your abilities to access the right hemisphere will enhance your appreciation of design in the theatre.

Design communication affects the audience's perceptions of the play in three primary ways: identification, clarification, and intensification. Design communicates basic information about the place of the dramatic action, the time period, the time of day, and the characters' functions or relationships to the plot of the play; this communication functions as *identification*. Design communicates complex information about the play's theme, the director's concept, the relationships of characters, the personalities of characters, and the style of the production; this communication functions as *clarification*. Finally design communicates emotional stimuli about the moods of the play, a scene, or a character, and about impact of a scene or character on an audience; this communication functions as *intensification*.

By looking at each type of design from an audience's point of view, your will understand *how* design communicates. As an audience member, you need to know how the language of design affects you. This knowledge will make you a better responder to design in the theatre.

Design and the Audience

Design's language is visual, aural, or kinesthetic. We understand its messages by processing the stimuli in the right hemisphere of the brain. To increase our accessibility to design's "language," we must understand *what* each type of design communicates and how it communicates in the theatre, i.e., the basic elements of design. Although this sounds complex, you already practice many of the skills needed. Your abilities to interpret and understand visual, aural, and kinesthetic stimuli is considerable.

What Does Design Communicate?

Set design identifies the place and time period of the production. Most often it will be the exact time and place defined by the playwright; sometimes directors may choose different locales and periods. Set design may create with considerable detail a specific environment: a living rooms, a hotel lobby, a restaurant, or a porch in a backyard. When a play demands more than one set, set designers will skillfully suggest a variety of locales and times, sometimes by just changing furniture or decoration on an almost bare stage. In these cases audiences must be flexible and adapt to the scenic changes as the production progresses.

Set design also clarifies the style of a production. Is the production realistic? If so, you will recognize the richness of detail which we associate with everyday life. Rooms will have walls, doors, staircases, carpets, furniture, and the decoration appropriate to that room. Stage properties will be real cups and saucers, glassware, ice cubes, food, and other functional objects. Is the production non-realistic? If so, you will be aware of the departures from ordinary reality: maybe exaggeration, like the larger than life scenery for musicals like *Guys and Dolls* will stretch your imaginations; maybe abstraction, like the unit sets often used in productions of Shakespeare's plays, will direct your focus to the language and characters.

Set design may clarify the ideas of a production. Both classical and modern playwrights offer viewpoints about the characters and their worlds. Set designers may visually represent these ideas to an audience. In Shakespeare's play *King John* the disintegration of King John and his kingdom is a major idea in the play. Designers have communicated this idea visually by showing the richness and elegance of the King and his court at the beginning disintegrating to tatters and rags by the end. Shakespeare's *Hamlet* has been designed to be played inside of a structure resembling a human skull, thereby emphasizing Hamlet's internal struggles. Design in musicals can often suggest important ideas: the outrageous decadence of the nightclub in *Cabaret* suggests the inner depravity of Germany in the 1930's.

Finally, set design can intensify the mood of a production. The seedy, spare motel room captures the grim intensity of the conflict in Sam Shepard's *Fool for Love*. The cold, forbidding hostile nature of the Antarctic emerges from the stark white barrenness of a set for Ted Tally's *Terra Nova*. The buildings, the laundry, the levels, the make-believe river, and the bountiful use of color project the joyful exuberance of *Scapino*.

Designers reflect different approaches to style in their work on three classic plays Liviu Ciulei's 1984 production of TWELFTH NIGHT by Shakespeare and Lucian Pintilie's 1984 production of Moliere's TARTUFFE at The Guthrie Theater, and the Shaw Festival's CAESAR AND CLEOPATRA by Bernard Shaw. (Courtesy of The Guthrie Theaer, Minneapolis, MN; photographs by Joe Giannetti. Courtesy of the Shaw Festival, Niagara-on-the-Lake, Ontario, Canada; photograph by David Cooper.)

Costume design gives the audience clues about the characters, as well as information about the time, place, and style of the play. Just as we judge people in everyday life by what they are wearing, in the theatre the audience develops perceptions about the characters through their costumes. Costume may reveal a character's occupation, age, financial condition, social status, and/or personality characteristics.

Also, costume tells the audience the time period of the play. Often we discern the specific period of the play—1600, 1800, 1920, or 1950—only through costume design. The place of the play's action is often revealed through costume: historic Greek or Roman costumes tell us as much about the play's locale as the scenery communicates. Finally, the costumes reinforce the play's style:the costumes in *Terra Nova* and *Fool for Love* encourage the audience toward a serious realism while the playfulness and exaggeration in *Guys and Dolls* suggest a larger-than-life comedic style.

Costume design also helps the director to control audience focus. A costume's color draws the audience's attention to a specific character. By placing the important character in

Desmond Heeley, designer for the 1988 THE GLASS MENAGERIE at The Guthrie Theater communicates the idea of shimmering fragility which is so much part of the play. Directed by Vivian Matalon, with David Ossian as Tom and Tracy Sallows as Laura. (Courtesy of The Guthrie Theater, Minneapolis, MN. Photograph by Michal Daniel.)

a bright color, or in a color which contrasts with the costume color of the other characters, the audience will focus on that character.

Finally, the costumes often help us to look at the two most communicative parts of an actor's body—the face and hands. Through the use of collars, cuffs, or scarfs of colors which contrast with the color of the rest of the costume, or through the use of jewelry, the costume designer encourages the audience to pay attention to the actor's face and hands.

Makeup design complements costume design to comment specifically on the character's age, personality, occupation, or health. All actors must wear makeup, because the lighting in theatre, film, or television is very intense. The lighting flattens the normal three-dimensional look of the face and turns the skin very pale. Makeup counteracts these effects of lighting, and makes actors look better on stage.

Set designer's Fritz Szabo's model for Iowa State University's TERRA NOVA represents a part of the designer's process. TERRA NOVA was directed by Gregg Henry, with costumes by Jane Cox and lighting by George Dowker. (Photograph by Mike Doolen.)

Makeup is either corrective or character. Corrective makeup improves actors' facial flaws and enhances their features. Character makeup changes actors' appearances to comment on some aspect of a character. Makeup tells the audience about characters, because faces are often reflections of self. The skin on the face reveals age: older skin loses its elasticity and hangs on the facial bones causing folds, bags, jowls, and lines. Jobs may show facially, e.g., a farmer's ruddy, weathered complexion contrasts with the smoother, softer pallor of the office worker. The lines around characters' mouths, eyes, and on their foreheads reflect their temperaments; laughter, frowns, impassivity, and pensiveness are

The starkly realistic TERRA NOVA as at Fisher Theater at Iowa State University (Courtesy of Iowa State University Theatre.)

written in characters' faces. Finally, in the theatre actors sometimes must resemble a family, reflecting the influence of heredity in how people look. The makeup design helps the audience develop its feelings and reactions to different characters during a production.

Lighting design illuminates both the actors and the play. In order to hear the dialogue and to understand the dramatic action, the audience must be able to see the faces of the characters. The actors' faces must look natural under the strong stage lights. Through a process called "modeling," the designer creates the natural three-dimensional quality of the face. Modeling provides sufficient illumination for the face and creates shadows to define features. The lights may also assist the audience in focusing on important characters or action. Audiences in the theatre must be guided where to look, and lighting dynamically helps the director achieve appropriate audience focus.

Lighting may communicate ideas and feelings about the play to the audience. Lighting tells us the time of day: dawn, morning, noon, sunset, or evening. Lighting enhances the

Technicians at The Guthrie Theater reassemble a turntable for the 1985 production of ANYTHING GOES. (Courtesy of The Guthrie Theater, Minneapolis, MN. Photograph by Timothy S. Streeter.)

mood of a scene. Appropriate lighting moves the audience to feelings of sadness, joy, exultation, coldness, or warmth. These effects are usually reinforcing the dominant mood found in a scene or demanded by the director. Lighting may suggest ideas; lights may magically cause characters to disappear, to die, or to appear from nowhere. Finally, lighting design coordinates with costume and set design to reveal the style of a production. For example, part of the pleasure of musicals is provoked by the joyously bright and colorful light, which enhances the larger-than-life style of many musicals.

Sound and music design intensifies the mood of a scene or play, and helps to identify the place of action or the time of day. Music stimulates strong emotional reactions in audiences without the interference of left brain cognition. In films musical scores support the dramatic action; this pervasive underscoring aids our involvement in the film's action. In the theatre music may be used before or during the action of the play. Directors often choose pre-show and intermission music to support the emotional textures of their productions, or to support the environment of the play, e.g., a play taking place in the 1950's using music associated with that time. During the action in a non-musical play, directors often add music at points to reinforce a mood or idea. Often playwrights of non-musical plays will have actually written a scene to include music as an integrated part of the dramatic ac-

Scenic artists use large paper stencils to paint the art deco carpeting for use in a scene from The Guthrie Theater's 1985 production of ANYTHING GOES. (Courtesy of The Guthrie Theater, Minneapolis, MN. Photograph by Timothy S. Streeter.)

tion. Only musicals, as a type of theatre, integrate music throughout to support the dramatic action.

Sound effects reinforce the visual elements of set and lighting to place the action and time of day. Hearing the chirruping of crickets evokes a summer evening; the sound of intense wind creates a unpleasant, cold feeling; and the noise of cars and horns suggests a city environment. Sound design draws us more deeply into the environment of the play.

How Does Design Communicate?

Design communicates by manipulating the elements of design to convey perceptions to an audience. We respond to the elements of design emotionally or cognitively, i.e., they stimulate feelings or thoughts within us. These emotions and thoughts reinforce our perceptions of a scene, character, or an entire play. Because the stimuli are primarily impacting the right hemisphere first, they have a powerful impact on how we respond to a production.

Design works to create the mood qualities in Iowa State University Theatre's FOOL FOR LOVE, directed by Patrick D. Gouran, set design by Wayne A. Mikos, costume design by Jane Cox, and lighting design by George Dowker. (Courtesy of Iowa State University Theatre. Photograph by Mike Doolen.)

A basic design element is *color*. Because set, lighting, and costume design use it, color may be the most powerful design element. In a production color comments on characters, ideas, and environments through specific cognitive and emotional responses internalized within each of us.

Audience members respond to color in two ways. Primary color association is cultural, i.e., influenced by the society and culture in which we were born and raised. In the United States typical color associations that we might have include:

- Red: Sexual, hot, outgoing, attention getting color.
- Pale blue: Cool, shy, conservative, relaxing color.
- White: Chastity; innocence, virtue; calm color.
- Black: Elegance; evil; sadness; mysterious color, the color of "loners".

Design captures the fun and exuberance of SCAPINO, produced by Iowa State University Theatre, with direction by Sarah Barker, set design by Erica Zaffarano, costume design by Jane Cox, and lighting design by Jill Rasmussen. (Courtesy of Iowa State University Theatre. Photography by Mike Doolen.)

These color associations are consistent throughout our culture. Therefore, designers can incorporate these colors into a visual design with predictable results.

Secondary color association is unpredictable, since it depends on our individual responses developed through association. For example, you may feel warm and comfortable whenever you see pale gray. As a primary color association, pale gray does not stimulate warmth. However, your particular association may result because your favorite grandmother who loved you so much as a child often wore pale gray. Such a secondary color association works just for you. Designers depend on the primary color associations.

The use of various colors affect our feelings toward the play and its characters. Costuming the wicked stepmother in red and black and Snow White in blue is a simple example of how color affects our perceptions. Set and lighting designers make similar choices. The vivid, vibrant, and optimistic color choices made for the sets and lighting of musicals like *Hello Dolly* contrast with the more somber, serious, and pessimistic choices

Costume plates are important parts of a designer's process. Wendy Collins' costume rendering for Feste in the 1986 Wisconsin Shakespeare festival production of TWELFTH NIGHT illustrates this art. (Photograph by Mike Doolen.)

made for a production of Arthur Miller's *Death of a Salesman.* Color in lighting can even encourage audiences to feel cold or heat: cool blue light suggests the sensation of cold, while hot oranges and red encourage warmth.

Color also directs our attention to a specific place on stage, to a particular character within a group, or even a specific part of a character's body. By arranging colors so that they contrast with each other, designers direct the audience's attention. Placing a red chair within a living room of earth tones, putting the main character in black at a party of whites and grays, or providing a white collar on a green dress will focus attention toward the contrasting color. In the case of the collar, costume designers often make this choice to draw focus to the actor's face.

Besides color designers utilize *form* as a design element as they build costumes and sets. Form is composed of two different design components—*line* and *mass;* together they

81

Wendy Collins' costume plate comes to life on Feste, played by Tom Loughlin, as he torments Malvolio, played by David P. Hirvela in the 1986 Wisconsin Shakespeare Festival production of TWELFTH NIGHT. (Courtesy of the Wisconsin Shakespeare Festival, Platteville, WI. Photograph by Andrew Baumann.)

combine to represent the form of three-dimensional objects, whether they be set pieces, furniture, or costumes.

The four different kinds of lines are represented in the illustration on p. 89.
Just as color has a cognitive or emotional impact on our senses, lines do also. Horizontal lines, because they encourage our eyes to move from left to right, create a feeling of stability and security, and a sense of endurance. We often surround ourselves in our homes, schools, and workplaces with objects composed of horizontal lines, e.g, sofas, desks, blackboards, and shelves.

Vertical lines, which move our eyes from the ground to the heavens, convey strength, majesty, power, might, or spirituality. For businessmen the pin-striped suit is a ''power'' choice. In architecture cathedrals capture the majesty and spirituality of our belief in God.

The curved line is relaxed, light-hearted, and happy. Curves appear in round conference tables (which suggest an equality and encourage positive interactions), beds shaped like hearts, and clothing that is full and maybe a bit large, which creates all kinds of curves as it hangs on the body.

Zig-zag lines, which make our eyes move back and forth erratically, are unsettling but exciting; they create feelings of uncertainty, nervousness, or chaos. Often these lines are created by disasters, e.g., the house devastated by fire, or earthquake or the destruction of war. Zig-zags would also occur in clothing that has been torn or ripped.

The mass of a piece of scenery or costume is its three dimensional bulk, size, or magnitude. A small mass suggests fragility and weakness, e.g., the three legged stool and shawl made of lace, while a large mass communicates power and force, e.g., the king's royal throne and the large black cape worn by villains like Count Dracula.

A design element exclusively the set designer's is *set decoration*. Set decoration consists of all the furniture and objects, called set properties, which appear on the completed set. These pieces not only utilize the design elements of color and form, but also make statements based on their style, condition, and quantity.

The style of furniture within a stage set speaks eloquently of the time, place, and personalities of the people living there. For example, a living room with Danish contemporary furniture gives a different feeling and attitude than one full of used furniture, orange crates, and book cases made of lumber and concrete blocks. The style of furniture also defines the time of a play, e.g., the elegance of 18th French furniture and set decoration places the time immediately. Of course, if this style of furniture decorates the room in contemporary times, we immediately can make some judgments about its owners.

The condition of the furniture and the objects speaks to the personalities of the owners. A room spotlessly clean and neatly arranged strikes us quite differently than one that is run-down and dirty.

Finally, the quantity of the furniture and decoration communicates qualities of the owners. A spare room with few objects decorating it or its walls creates a different feeling than a room crammed with furniture and overflowing with decorative objects and paintings on the walls.

The lighting designer has three other powerful design elements besides color: *distribution*, *intensity*, and *movement*. The designer controls how light is distributed on the stage in three ways—its direction, its shape and size, and its quality. The designer chooses the lighting instrument, which may produce a diffuse distribution of light or a sharply defined distribution. The size of this instrument will determine the shape and size of the light it produces. Where the designer hangs the instrument determines the direction of the light. Color and intensity affect the quality of the light, and the cognitive and emotional values it has for an audience.

The intensity of light, i.e., its relative brightness or dimness, is another controllable quality of light. Through the use of a lighting control board, a designer can provide lighting instruments from 100% to 5% of their full power.

Costumes reflect the style and period of two different productions of the Shaw festival, PRIVATE LIVES by Noel Coward; and CYRANO DE BERGERAC by Edmond Rostand, and The Guthrie Theater's THE IMPORTANCE OF BEING ERNEST by Oscar Wilde (Courtesy of the Shaw Festival and The Guthrie Theater. Guthrie photograph by Joe Giannetti.)

Finally, lights move either physically or in timed intervals. We are aware of how stage lights change as scenes shift or productions begin or end. The lighting designer controls these movements of light to affect audience's perceptions. The spotlight which follows the lead singer in a musical illustrates actual physical movement of light. Distribution, intensity, and movement affects the audience's thoughts and emotions as a play progresses before our eyes.

Music and sound design have a powerful impact on the right hemisphere, and on our perceptions as we experience a play production. The explanation of how they achieve their impact is completely explained in the chapter devoted to an audience's appreciation of music.

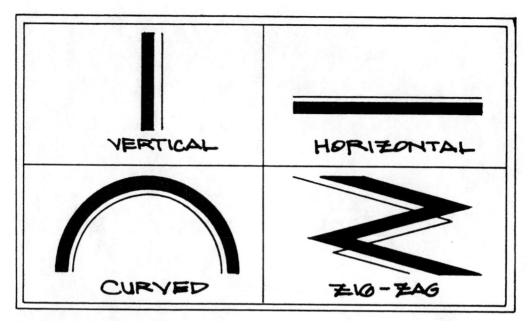

Four Types of Line. (Illustration by Fritz Szabo.)

The Importance of Design

Design exerts a powerful impact on the audience's visual and aural perceptions. Rather than merely existing to provide attractive environments and costumes for actors, design contributes significantly to the communication of the ideas and emotions expressed by the playwright through the actors. The verbal ideas that we are hearing will be reinforced visually by design in a theatrical production which is unified in its conceptual approach. The theatre artist who provides the unity of vision is the director.

Direction

Play production demands interaction among a variety of theatre artists, who bring their individual interpretive skills to the interpretive art of theatre. These artists communicate indirectly to the audience the meaning of the play, that revelation of truth about human behavior represented in the playwright's words. For the communication to have meaning within this collaborative, interpretive, and indirect art, any production must give the audience a unified vision of the play. The director provides this vision.

The director is a relative newcomer to theatrical production. The over 2000 year history of theatre notes the director's arrival as a theatre artist in the late 19th century. Up to

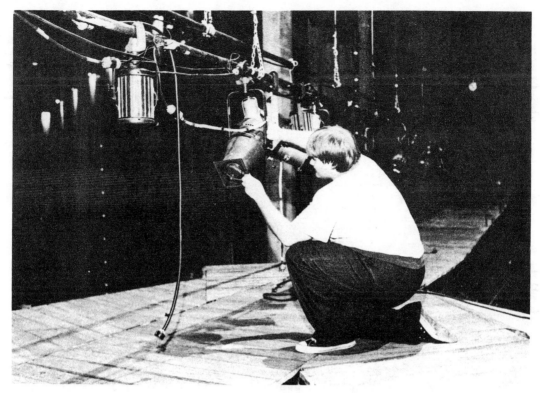

Student lighting technician adjusts a lighting instrument during a light hang. (Courtesy of Iowa State University Theatre. Photograph by Mike Doolen.)

the 1860's and 1870's playwrights, actors, or actor-managers, had made many of the decisions directors face today. However, because our world and theatre technology have become more complex, the director's role has grown in importance as the unifying, interpretive force in today's theatre. The hierarchy of any production places the director at the top of the decision-making structure. The director is the person ultimately responsible for the success or failure of any production.

As we attend plays or musicals, we are consciously aware of the play and the actors; our interest in human behavior causes us to relate emotionally and cognitively with the story of the play and the characters, fleshed out by actors. The visual/aural impact of design gives us additional excitement, information, and pleasure. However, audiences rarely notice the person ultimately responsible for the whole experience—the director, the ''invisible person'' in the theatre experience.

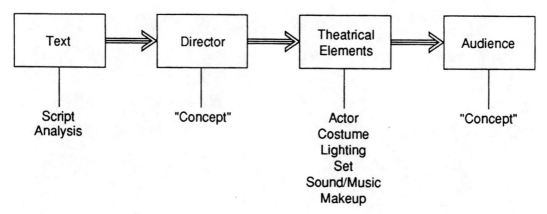

The Director's Communication Model.

The Director's Impact on the Audience

The director's role in today's theatre is complex and varied, reflecting a variety of tasks performed during the typical production process. A director plays many roles including those of an interpreter, a coordinator, an acting teacher, an evaluator, a communicator, and a psychologist. Although all the director's roles are visible in the final production, the audience notices most the role of "interpreter."

As an interpreter a director provides unity for the production and audience focus. The unity of artistic vision in a theatrical production is called the "concept", or "production concept" ; sometimes it is referred to as the "director's concept." Focus refers to directorial choices that lead the audience to look at and listen to the primary action in the present moment of a production. Within these two goals as an interpreter are many tasks which have direct impact on the audience.

Development of the Production Concept

The director's most important audience-related task is the development of the production concept, which unifies all the theatrical elements. What is the production concept? Simply, it is what the director wants the audience to get from a production; what the audience should walk away with in their thoughts and feelings. The concept unifies a production because it is an expression of the play's meaning that is translated into theatrical terms. It should be the essence of the play, easily communicated in words and images to the actors and designers, who will communicate the concept to the audience through their arts.

The Director's Communication Model diagrams the evolution of a production concept. The text should be the source for production concepts. Directors find their production concepts through script analysis, a detailed evaluation of the script from the points of view of dramatic action, characters, and idea. What the director "finds" in script analysis is the core meaning of the play. Sometimes a play's theme or central idea captures a director's

This composition from the Shaw Festival's 1985 production of HEARTBREAK HOUSE, directed by Christopher Newton, establishes a strong sense of relationship between Capt. Shotover, played by Douglas Rain, and Ellie Dunn, played by Marti Maraden. (Courtesy of the Shaw Festival. Photograph by David Cooper.)

imagination; sometimes it's the emotions engendered by the characters and dramatic action; and sometimes it's the spectacle encouraged by the text. Whatever the director wants the audience to receive from the production is the "production concept." The director must be able to state this concept clearly, because throughout the production process the concept will be held up as the goal for designers and actors to follow. Ideally, if director, actors, and designers have done their jobs, the audience will leave the theatre having perceived the production concept. As the director's point of view about a text, the concept can only reach an audience indirectly through the work of actors and designers.

Implementation of the Production Concept

At any given moment in a theatre production, you as an audience member are able to look at anything within the theatre environment: at actors talking, at scenery, at costumes, at your program, or even at the person sitting next to you. For the production concept to have impact on your senses and your mind, the director must guide your focus at any given present moment in the theatre. The film director has an easier job in guiding audience's

This composition from The Guthrie Theater's 1981 production of FOXFIRE, directed by Marshall Mason, clearly establishes Dillard's strong audience focus. He is closest to the audience of the three characters, and has the eye focus of Hector and Annie Nations. (Courtesy of The Guthrie Theater. Photograph by Bruce Goldstein.)

focus; if the director wants you to focus on the leading woman's eyes, the camera will move in for a close-up on her eyes. As an audience member you have no choice but to look at her eyes; they fill the screen having the desired impact that the director wants. In the theatre the director's task is more difficult. Since you control where you look on stage, a director will want to structure the experience so that your focus will be on whatever is important to the communication of the production concept.

The director has specific tools to help guide focus. By using composition, movement, and gesture of actors a director creates a plan for controlling audience focus. Directors often call this plan the *blocking* for the play.

Any action by an actor seen by an audience is part of blocking. This action includes: movement—the moments when actors are in transit from one location on stage to another; composition—the pictures created by stationary actors; and gesture—all the physical action actors might do while stationary with their faces or bodies.

90

Simply stated, blocking is the movement, composition, and gestures that make up the visual aspect of actor-audience communication. Movement and composition are directorial functions; gesture is an actor function, which should always complement the director's intent.

There is an old theatre saying: "The eye is quicker than the ear." It means that the audience will look at the character who is moving, making movement a useful and effective tool for focusing audience attention.

The usual practice is that the actor with the line has the movement. Since the lines most often carry the dramatic action, the director wants to focus attention on the character who is speaking to aid the audience's understanding of the play. Ninety-five percent of the time actors move on their lines. The exceptions are when a director deliberately wants the audience to watch some specific action or to concentrate on a non-speaking character. The non-speaking, moving actor will draw attention from the stationary, speaking one.

Movement can be executed in a variety of tempos. Directors set the tempo according to the character's desires at that moment. Fast crosses, for instance, might suggest impulsiveness, fear, surprise, lack of control; slow crosses might suggest deliberation, strength, control, insecurity, reflection. By controlling the tempo of movement directors communicate to audiences emotional qualities about characters and dramatic action.

Compositions are pictures created by stationary actors. The audience interprets living pictures the same way we interpret painted pictures—attributing emotional values to the figures in the painting and drawing conclusions from the relationships among the figures. Composition, as a directorial tool, can communicate dramatic action as effectively as movement.

Types of compositions depend on the distances between the characters. In close compositions, characters are actually touching or are just a foot apart. Such compositions communicate climactic emotional confrontations: love, hate, anger. Moderate compositions, with characters seated or standing two to three feet apart, are the norm in most productions. They are most effective when characters are in agreement. Finally, in distant compositions, the characters are more than three feet apart. The greater the distance between the characters, the greater the suggested emotional distance. Distant compositions imply lack of care and concern for other characters, and communicate serious emotional or intellectual disagreement.

Directors have great flexibility in making their living pictures communicate to audience. Within the three basic types of compositions, the director may manipulate the following elements of composition: actor body positions, vertical levels, placement of characters in relation to the audience, placement of characters in relation to each other, control of eye focus of characters on stage.

A director can control the audience's focus of attention by using movement, and the various types and elements of composition. Blocking also makes interpretational statements about character and relationship qualities (e.g., dominance or submissiveness) and emotional qualities (e.g., grief, joy, anger). Also, by controlling focus, the director helps the audience receive all the verbal and visual signals important to the dramatic action of the play. By increasing understanding, directors enhance the audience's enjoyment of the production.

Directors also guide the audience's focus through their communication with actors and designers. In rehearsals the director influences actors to make vocal, physical, and emotional choices which clarify characters' wants and objectives in relation to the production concept. Also, directors affect designers' choices of color; form; furniture; lighting direction, intensity, and movement; and makeup. The design elements working with the director's blocking guide audience focus. The director's work with actors and designers is less immediately visible to the audience. Yet, the invisible hand guiding your focus in the theatre audience is that of the director indirectly communicating.

Conclusion

The magic of theatre occurs when all the creative artists collaborate to whisk you away from the everyday world to the world of the play. If you find your willing suspension of disbelief engaged, so that you are actively participating in the aesthetic reality of *Hamlet* or *Annie* or *The Glass Menagerie*, then the playwright, the actors, the designers, and the director have achieved their goals as performing artists. Understanding the language of the theatre is the first step toward your greater appreciation of this performing art.

CHAPTER 5

Music

No other performing art immediately touches our thoughts and emotions as music. In concert halls and arenas, at home and in our cars, no day goes by without music flooding our ears with those special sounds of jazz, rock, classical, country/western, or "easy listening" music. Because of modern technology, we may respond to music anywhere. Radio, cassette players, stereo equipment, CD players, or walkmen bring music to us wherever and whenever we want it. Music is everywhere.

Music pervades the other performing arts. Opera and musicals are special types of theatre. Musical sound tracks are crucial to our response to film. TV uses musical sound tracks, besides devoting programs or complete networks (MTV) to the presentation of music. Music stimulates the dancer's body to move. Radio devotes 90% of its regular programming to music.

Music appeals to everyone. As an performing art it has universal appeal. No one dislikes music. People may express a preference for a certain type of music, but no one rejects music totally. From the past as three year olds when we danced to the beat of the music, to the present when we sit and listen to a musical group play, music remains a positive, exciting force our lives.

Sources of Music's Appeal

Music's universal appeal was recognized by Plato, Greek philosopher and one of Western civilization's greatest thinkers, in his book, *The Republic*. In the book Plato recognized the power of music in the soul. Allan Bloom in *The Closing of the American Mind* sums up Plato's teaching about music:

> Plato's teaching about music is, put simply, that rhythm and melody, accompanied by dance, are the barbarous expression of the soul. Barbarous, not animal. Music is the medium of the human soul in its most ecstatic condition of wonder and terror... Music is the soul's primitive and primary speech... without articulate speech or reason. It is not only not reasonable, it is hostile to reason. Even when articulate speech is added, it is utterly subordinate to and determined by the music and the passions it expresses. (p. 71)

Plato's correct analysis of the lack of rational control over the influence of music recognizes the difference between the right and left hemispheres of the brain.

Music affects our sensibilities directly through the right hemisphere of the brain. Music appeals without reference to verbal, analytical, cognitive, and/or linear thinking. Our response to music does not need the dominant left hemisphere. Music's appeal is non-verbal. Even in songs, where lyrics—words joined to music—are an essential ingredient, the non-verbal elements of music are usually dominant. The lyrics almost function as aids to remember the melody.

Because music's appeal is non-verbal, you might say that "we don't have to think about it." In the sense that we equate "thinking" with only left brain activities and in the sense that Plato defined "reasoning," music does not demand thinking. As an art audiences can respond to music, using primarily their right hemispheres, without a need for "thoughts" about what they are hearing. This quality of direct acquisition of the elements of music *without* having to figure out what it means gives music a universal appeal.

Music's effect on our emotions also strengthens its universality. Music communicates emotion. It can stimulate feelings within us directly and immediately. For example, we all have been cheered up or moved to tears just by hearing a specific piece of music. Sometimes this phenomenon is caused by association of the music to a particular event in our lives. However, often the music itself provokes the response: its melody, tone color, rhythm, harmony, or form. This emotional response also supports the importance of the right hemisphere in receiving the stimuli of music as a performing art.

Understanding the basis for music's universal appeal leads us to answering the question—what is the meaning of music? Often as we listen to unfamiliar or difficult music that question pops into our minds. And, most often, we use our left hemispheres to try to figure out an answer. However, since most music is written to communicate pure emotions, meaning in music is seldom something you can express in words. Therefore, the left hemisphere will fail in its attempt to find what music means. The right hemisphere provides the answer to the question. By listening to what is going on inside you and by being responsive to your feelings, you will find the meaning in any music. Meaning in music is internal, not external.

The conductor of the Leningrad State Symphony, Alexander Dmitriev, inspires the musicians in performance. (Courtesy of ICM Artists, Ltd.)

Music Appreciation and Listening

The ubiquity of music and the ease with which we respond has a negative side for us, the vast audience, of this performing art. Many of us have lost the ability to listen to music. The recording arts make music so available that it is almost omnipresent in our lives—from the music we choose to listen to in our homes, our cars, and on portable tape players to the music that is piped into our offices, shopping centers, stores, and elevators. These daily musical stimuli may pass unnoticed in our minds as we think about other things. Certainly merely ''hearing'' music does not lead to greater aesthetic appreciation.

Many of us are quite narrow-minded about music. We like classical music but hate other kinds. We like rock music but refuse to listen to classical music. Whatever our preferences the source of our prejudices is the ''monster'' of responding negatively to anything unfamiliar. If your total musical experience is with rock music, every other kind of music is strange, unknown, unfamiliar. Human beings tend to respond negatively to anything that they do not know. Since all music is composed of the same basic elements, elements which we respond to in our favorite music, with more knowledge we can expand our present taste in music.

Another source of our narrow-mindedness may be that we really have never learned how to listen to music. We may think that hearing and listening are the same thing. We may assume that everyone is born with the ability to listen to music. The process of listening to music demands knowing why you listen to music and developing skills to enhance your present ability to listen. By improving your listening, you will enhance the experience of music.

Basic Elements of Music

The basic elements of music, i.e., what makes up music as we recognize it, are the same whether we are listening to Beethoven's *Fifth Symphony,* Duke Ellington's "Take the A Train," or the Rolling Stones' "I Can't Get No Satisfaction." By knowing the elements of music, listeners become more aware of the similarities between all types of music, which may help to break down prejudices against unfamiliar types. Also, knowledge of the elements gives a focus for your listening and opens your perceptions to what in the music may be the stimulus for your response. Finally, we must recognize that the basic elements stimulate our emotional response to music.

Melody is the element of music you are responding to when you find yourself whistling or humming a bit of music. Melody is the tune, or more technically the sequence of single tones which produce a whole; the whole is the tune. Melodies can be as simple as the tune to the song "Happy Birthday," or as complex as a movement in a symphony. Melodies may vary in length, and usually will be repeated as part of the selection of music. Audiences like the repetition of melody. This repetition, sometimes with changes in the character of melody, is a hallmark of all music—from popular songs to string quartets.

Rhythm is the "beat" of music. We respond to rhythm by tapping our feet; by moving our fingers, hands, or head; by conducting an "imaginary" orchestra; or by dancing. Dancing is a organized physical expression of our response to rhythm in music. Rhythm is the physical aspect of music. It works hand-in-hand with melody. Rhythm's power is very persuasive. Even the most avid detractor of rock music finds it difficult to listen to this contemporary music without moving some part of the body.

Tone color in music refers to the character of the sound, which distinguishes one instrument from another. A melody may be represented by single instrument, e.g., a piano, or a voice, e.g., a soprano, or several instruments, e.g., an orchestra. Depending on the instrumentation, the melody will have a particular character to its sound which encourages specific feelings toward the melody. Often the melody is repeated using different instruments or voices, each repeat causing a change in the quality of the sound. This character of the sound is tone color. Our awareness of the unique blending of instruments and voices, or of the distinct impact of a single voice or instrument as the melody progresses is our sensitivity to tone color. Composers and musicians recognize tone color's effect on our response to music, and make conscious aesthetic choices in the instrumentation for a piece of music.

Harmony is difficult to explain in words, but easy to identify when you are listening to music. Harmony is the simultaneous sounding of two or more notes, especially when they are pleasing to the ear. A clear example of harmony is the barbershop quartet. Four distinct tone colors—first and second tenor, baritone, and bass—sounding four different notes which create a pleasing whole to our ears. Harmony can be found in all types of music. And, sometimes contemporary composers may choose to create disharmonies in order to communicate particular feelings for their music.

Finally, all music has *form* as a basic element. The form of music is the organizational structure imposed upon melody, rhythm, harmony, and tone color. Music exists in various forms or *genres:* song, symphony, sonata, opera, concerto, quartet, overture, musical, operetta, hymn, cantata, mass, oratario, and march just to name a few. Each genre can be divided into smaller forms, just as a play can be divided into acts, and further divided into scenes. The diversity of forms may appear overwhelming to the general listener of music. How will I ever understand form when so many exist and each one has its own complexities and variations? Certainly to become a musician or a music specialist, knowledge of musical genres is important. However, to improve your listening to music, you only must know how form influences your response to music.

Form often provides the sense of completion that we feel when a musical selection ends. Music moves through a basic pattern of tension-relaxation. The music builds in tension, then releases the tension. This pattern repeats through a musical form. The end of the music brings the sense of completion. No matter what the specific form, we usually receive a feeling of satisfaction, if not elation, from the completion of a work of music. You can test yourself on this issue. Listen to a cassette, record, or CD and stop a musical selection half way through its playing. Your profound sense of dissatisfaction is your response to the interruption of the form of the music. Some composers choose for a specific aesthetic purpose to leave the audience in the state of unreleased tension. Understanding form will prepare you for whatever the composer desires.

When you combine your knowledge of the elements of music with specific methods of enhancing your listening to music, you increase your chances of appreciating any kind of music more. Melody, rhythm, tone color, harmony, and form are not just cognitive concepts, but are crucial to your enjoyment of music as you listen. The goal of increasing your knowledge of music's basic elements is to integrate them into your active music listening. With this information about music's components we can make active choices as we listen which reinforce music's primary appeal to the emotions, and which increase our appreciation.

How to Improve Music Listening

Responding to music as a performing art may require a major behavioral change in how you listen to music. As mentioned earlier, for many of us listening to music is merely the act of "hearing" it. We passively accept the sounds as they enter our brains, and think no more about it. We may even be unaware of hearing music or recognizing the selection of music.

However, before exploring ways to improve music listening, audiences must know why they are listening to music. Our purpose in listening affects how we actually listen. Understanding your purpose in listening to music is the first step in improving your music listening.

Why Do You Listen to Music?

The following descriptions of people listening to music illustrate major reasons why we listen to music. See how many of these illustrations capture your music listening experience.

> As Bill studied for his Botany exam, his room was filled with the sounds of classical music. His concentration focused clearly on the structure of leaves.

> Walking across campus, Sue thought of how great her homecoming weekend would be. She was wafted along with tunes from classic Beatles hits from the headset of her Walkman.

> The young mother washed and diapered her baby girl, smiling and talking to her, hardly aware of the radio in the background playing the latest rock song.

We often use music to go along with other activities. Our focus is not particularly on the music, but on doing other things, e.g., studying, daydreaming, walking, daily activities. When we use music this way, clearly we are not listening to it; it merely provides a pleasant, audible background for our primary activity.

> The party roared to life as the rock tune blasted from the stereo system, surely rattling the china in the house next door. Couples danced their hearts away, while those on the sidelines moved to the overwhelming beat of the music.

Music is a stimulus to dance. In planning social events we anticipate our desires to dance by having music going before guests arrive for a party. We often find ourselves moving our bodies to music in unexpected situations, e.g., as we are driving down an Interstate or attempting to work in an office. A purpose in listening to music may be simply that you feel like dancing.

> As the rock music filled the junior high school gym, some girls dragged reluctant boys to the dance floor. Laughter and chatter bubbled forth incessantly. The music bonded the

13 year olds, and separated them from the faculty and parents chaperoning this school dance.

As you joined in the hymn, "A Mighty Fortress is Our God," you felt a kinship and a fellowship with the members of your church congregation. Singing hymns made you feel close to them and your religion.

Music allows you to feel closer to those people who share your interests. It serves as a bond to connect you to one another. Whether the interests are religious, social, artistic, or political (note the use of music in political campaigns or social movements) music can bring together those of like interests. Often this opportunity to associate with those who share your interests is a strong reason to listen to music.

As "Moon River" starts, David remembers that special evening with Jeannie. The warmth of their relationship and the happiness of their moments together rush over him.

Worn out from work, John puts "Old Time Rock and Roll Music" on the stereo. As he dances and plays "air guitar" to the song, his spirits become lighter. He loses some fatigue and gains energy to face the evening.

People listen to music to remember pleasant times from the past, or to stimulate a change in their moods. Music has the incredible power to do both. Since particular music is often associated with specific events in our lives, just listening to the music brings back those memories, e.g., for many of us Christmas music possesses this power. And, just as music may induce pleasant memories, it may stimulate us to change our mood. In fact collections of music are available which promise to relax us and reduce tension. These reasons of recalling memories or changing moods are valid purposes to listen to music.

The overture from Mozart's *Don Giovanni* filled the auditorium. Allan, bathed in sounds from his favorite composer, was at the same time refreshed and invigorated by the music. The music moved his mind to emotions and ideas stimulated by Mozart.

Escaping to the smoky, laidback jazz club was a Friday night pleasure for Donna. She loved moving to the rhythms and experiencing the emotions stimulated by jazz. All this was so far away from the world of office and family.

Music listening can provide us ways of escaping the everyday routine of living. Attending a music performance—whether it be a classical music concert, a jazz performance, or a rock concert—is a special event apart from our everyday existence. A performance may also encourage emotional or aesthetic involvement with the work of musicians and composers. When we listen to music with these purposes, we have the opportunity to enlarge our experience of life.

Listening to music with the wrong purpose could affect your enjoyment of the experience. For example, attending a concert with the background of only listening to music as an accompaniment to other activities would make you a very impatient listener. At concerts—especially those of classical music—the major activity is listening, not doing something else.

Music as a performing art usually demands a willingness to listen so that your emotions and thoughts are engaged with the music. Other goals in listening may be operative, but listening with full sensitivity to the experience is essential.

How to Improve Your Listening to Music

Most people somehow do not feel qualified to listen to music with empathy and full sensitivity to the experience. Maybe the lack of musical training affects our cognitive process in dealing with music; we feel inadequate to understand such a complex and mysterious art. Maybe we feel that non-popular music is only accessible to the few who understand classical music genres, the composers, the time in which the music was written, and/or the special jargon associated with it, e.g., scherzo, allegro, piano, forte, C major, *ad infinitum*. Maybe we feel insecure in a concert hall experience; what should we be thinking as the music fills our ears?

These responses are adequate rationalizations for excluding any "strange and different" musical experience from our lives. All of the rationalizations incorrectly perceive the music listening experience.

Music training is crucial to the performance of music, and enhances its appreciation as an art form. Giving yourself opportunities to practice an art, even on an elementary level, increases your insight. However, music training is not crucial to the act of listening to music. Your present musical tastes do not depend on your ability to play the music. We like rock music not because we all can play electric guitar, or operate a music synthesizer. We relate to the music we like because it is familiar to us, and because we "tune in" to the basic elements of music.

Familiarity first determines our tastes in music. If we have listened to a particular type of music over the years, we "know" it; it becomes like an old friend; it can be relied upon to bring us certain satisfactions. This is especially true in our response to contemporary music. It has surrounded our lives from our earliest memories; it bonds us to our friends; we associate social occasions from beach parties to dances to concerts with contemporary music. Most young people (really anyone who grew up after the early 1950's!) feel relaxed and comfortable in responding to it. People, who were introduced to classical music or jazz or Broadway showtunes when they were growing up, feel the same comfort with their favorite musical styles.

This relaxed attitude when listening to familiar music opens your right hemisphere to responding to the elements of music. When you are listening to contemporary music, for example, you are not thinking about the meaning of the music or the correct response to what you are hearing. On the contrary, you are sensorially involved in the experience: humming or singing the melody, moving to the rhythm, listening to the sounds of different instruments or voices, letting your body "feel" the music, and moving with the "emotions" in the music, playing imaginary musical instruments, or watching the musicians as they play. This natural behavior in your listening to your favorite kind of music is exactly the correct listening behavior when faced with any music listening experience.

Analyzing your behavior when you are really responding to your favorite music reveals several important attitudes toward music listening. You never doubt your ability to listen, i.e., no thought enters your mind that you might not be able to respond to this music listening experience. You trust your ability to listen. This particular attitude is the key to all effective music listening. When you are confident of your listening, you relax and process the stimuli appropriately using primarily your right hemisphere. You respond to music in the natural way, i.e., without cluttering the process with left hemisphere analysis and desires to "make sense" of every moment.

Knowledge about music (e.g., performance experience, understanding of the basic elements, historical knowledge, or information about a particular selection) can be useful to enhancing appreciation beyond the level of sensorial, comfortable listening. In fact the more you listen, the more musical knowledge you want to accumulate. However, as useful as this knowledge is to growth in understanding more about music, it is not necessary to promoting effective listening to music performance. Since our response to music is internal (i.e., how it affects our feelings) and is not to be found externally in the music itself, the techniques of effective listening in everyday life promote the best approaches to music listening.

Just like listening in everyday life, listening to music demands more than just using your ears. Music is more than an aural experience. Certainly aural stimuli are integral to music listening, but we listen with our other senses, too. Touch and sight aid our total experience. Also, our physical responses to the feelings generated by the music help in listening. Observe your response to your favorite music. You may already practice these listening techniques.

Practical Techniques to Improve Music Listening

Keep awareness in the present moment. Audience members must keep attention in the present moment. This means concentrating on what is happening to you and your senses in the immediate moment. We must avoid left hemisphere attempts to analyze and evaluate the music at the moment it is being performed. Our right hemispheres must remain open to the sensations of the music and the emotions which the music stimulates. Present moment concentration prevents daydreaming or worry. Using your mind's visualization power in relation to the music is appropriate and encouraged as an approach to responding to music; this technique will be discussed later. Finally, concert goers must steel themselves against any external distractions. Responding to music is primarily an internal activity, and you must minimize the influence of external listening distractions, e.g., talking audience members, poor seats, an overheated auditorium, or late arrivals.

EXERCISE: You can practice keeping your concentration in the present moment, and with practice can lengthen your "living" in present moments. Simply lie down or relax in a comfortable chair. Let your muscular tensions flow from your body as you sink into the floor, bed, or chair. If you feel any tensions, move those muscles slightly, to work them out. Now, for as long as you can, keep your thoughts in the present moment; think only thoughts that relate to what is happening to you *now*. If you slip into thoughts dealing with the past or future, or which evaluate this exercise, take control of your thoughts again and bring them back to the present moment. See how long you can keep your thoughts in the present. See if you can lengthen the amount of time that your thoughts are in the present.

This exercise is harder than it first appears. We spend much of our present moment thinking worrying about the future or fretting about the past or daydreaming about what might have been. However, since we do control our thoughts, we can increase our minds' abilities to stay in the present moment. During the exercise you probably were aware how much you depended on your senses to keep you in the present moment. Techniques to improve music listening fully utilize our senses.

This present moment exercise can be practiced *with music*. Play some music—preferably something that you are not familiar with. Get into the same relaxed position. As you are listening to the music, keep your concentration on the present moment, which is now filled with music. Keep your thoughts dealing with only what is happening now. The following suggestions should develop further your abilities to concentrate on the present moment in music listening.

Use your eyes to help your listening. Our visual sense helps in two ways in listening to music. What we are seeing in the present moment of a musical performance can be helpful to our hearing the music. Watching musicians focuses, rather than distracts from our attention on the music. In watching a quartet, band, or orchestra, we actually see the sound of the music move from section to section, or from instrument to instrument. This visually reinforces our perception of the music. Also, watching musicians increases our empathy with them as they perform. Their emotions in creating the music are visually and physically conveyed to the audience. This empathy supports the emotions of the music.

Our visual sense also allows us to create pictures in our minds. We can close our eyes and see whatever we want to see in our imaginations. Your imagination can create its own images in response to the music. In a way you use the music to score your own movie, visualized at the moment of listening. For some audience members their own imaginations stimulated by the music provide a satisfying beginning to music listening.

Either way of using your eyes will enhance your listening. Both help to internalize the process of music listening. Both can best be practiced when listening to a live musical performance. Imagination assists in reaction to recorded music.

As your knowledge of music increases, you naturally use visualization less. Music becomes an art to be appreciated aesthetically. You focus on its aesthetic elements and your internal responses to them, rather than creating visualizations to support music's stimuli. This natural development should not deter your use of imagination as you start concentrated music listening.

Use your physical reactions to the music. Physical reactions refer to any bodily response while listening to music: tapping your feet, moving your head or arms, tapping

Rehearsal is an essential part of preparation for performance. Joseph Christensen prepares the Iowa State University Wind Ensemble. (Courtesy of Iowa State University Information Services. Photograph by Pete Krumhardt.)

your fingers. These bodily responses help your listening, because they are absolute manifestations that you are internalizing the music. As you watch musicians perform, note how they are physically responding to the music; they are physically feeling the music as it is happening.

If you find that your past experience or social conditioning restrains your physical response to music, practice in private may increase your responses. When alone listen to a selection of unknown music. Allow it to infect your muscles; move yourself with the music. This exercise can be done standing, sitting, or lying down. Exaggerate your physical response to the music. If you find this difficult, repeat the exercise with a familiar piece of music; you should find this easier to physically move to. Avoid dancing, although you might really feel like dancing. Now return to the unknown music, and ride the music like a surfer rides an ocean wave. Play along with the musicians physically, or actually conduct the music as if you were the conductor of a symphony orchestra.

When you are in a concert hall listening to a concert, you will not be able to bounce around the hall as you may have in your own bedroom. However, any physical response to the music in the present moment will add to your music listening abilities.

Use your ears without analyzing or evaluating. Our dominant left-hemisphere often interferes with music listening by wanting to analyze or evaluate the experience at the moment it is happening. Of course this modifies our reception of the music. Choosing activities that the left hemisphere rejects will help you to avoid this problem. Concentrate on the sounds of the music—melodies, harmonies, tone color. Often this is assisted by listening to individual instruments as they make their entrances and additions to the piece of music. Remember that these sounds have no external meaning, but only the meaning that they stimulate within you as you listen. If your left-brain insists ("I don't understand what this means!"), return your focus to the sounds of the music and the individual instruments.

Conclusion

When all of these listening techniques are used together and in conjunction with your knowledge of music, you increase your chances of engaging yourself with the music experience. By enhancing your music listening capability, you will feel the emotions and grow in your appreciation of music.

CHAPTER 6

Dance

People have always loved to dance. From the earliest times when dance was part of the sacred rituals of primitive religions to the present when aerobics helps our physical fitness, dance has been part of civilization. We may use dance for personal pleasure and relaxation. Or, dance may be at the center of our social activities, whether we dance at private parties, or nightclubs, or formal occasions. Today people dance for many reasons.

Professional dancers have another purpose for dance: artistic interpretation. Dance as artistic interpretation is performance art and demands an audience. This type of dancing is often called theatrical dance, implying the need for a performance space and an audience to achieve its purposes. Theatrical dance may often puzzle and/or alienate us. Looking at dance as audience members rather than as participants, we are unsure how to respond. What does it mean? What are the dancers trying to communicate? What should my response be? These left-brain demands many times dampen our spontaneous reactions and leave us feeling unsatisfied with dance as performance art.

Like the preceding chapters, this one will focus on understanding the basics of dance as a performing art; the language of dance, i.e., how it communicates; and the specific actions you can choose as audience members to enhance your reception of dance as a performing art.

Basic Elements of Dance

To dance all you need is the human body. The essence of dance as a performing art is the human body and its potential: its abilities to move, its physical condition, and its training, all of which make certain movements possible and aesthetic are the body's potentials. The most elemental response to dance as performance art recognizes the dancers' bodies and the ways in which they move.

However, dance is more than movement, more than even rhythmic and expressive movement. We can achieve both by walking every day. And, dance is more than merely possessing a physically conditioned body. Many people have a well-conditioned body, but do not presume that they are dancers. What are the basic elements of this performance art so dependent on the human body and its potentials?

Dancers usually do not create a performance spontaneously, i.e., most theatrical dance is choreographed and rehearsed rigorously before audiences see it. Choreography is a plan for the movements in a dance created by a choreographer, who responds to a specific piece of music, rhythmic sounds, words being read aloud, or simply an idea. Choreography captures the mind and body, the ideas and feelings of the choreographer, who transforms them into visual kinetic patterns we call dance.

Choreographers are similar to play directors, with the important exception that the final dance performance is the choreographer's individual and original creation; play directors interpret the work of playwrights rather than create whole plays from scratch. However, some dance concerts are recreations of someone else's original choreography; in these cases the original choreographer usually is credited in the publicity and program of the concert. Choreographers, who are usually former dancers, understand and utilize the elements of dance, and communicate them to dancers.

The dancers interpret the choreography using the human body and its potentials. The dancers using the basic elements of dance reveal the feeling, form, or idea of the dance to the audience. The most basic elements of dance are *time, space,* and *energy. How* the dancers use these elements create the interpretation and the form of the dance.

Time for dancers exists primarily in rhythms, i.e., regular recurring beats which are part of music or can be created as simply as clapping the hands. The rhythm of a dance performed in silence may be the dancer's own breaths. Rhythms are affected by tempos—slow to fast. If choreographers choose to use music, they make decisions about how to respond to different speeds of rhythmic patterns. Dancers use their bodies as the instrument of response to rhythm. Heads, shoulders, torsos, arms, hips, legs, and feet may be involved individually, or in concert with each other. Rhythm may also be expressed in movement; walking, running, jumping, leaping, rolling, or tumbling may capture the dominant rhythms and tempos.

Space to the choreographer or dancer is like a canvas to the painter. Just as a painter fills a canvas with various colors and forms, choreographers and dancers fill space with movements utilizing different rhythms and energies. The space most often used is that of a stage, that three dimensional cube of space which audience members look at. Choreographers fill the space with dancers—either alone, in couples, or in larger groups—to communicate the designs or feelings inherent in their choreography.

Energy in dance is the amount of force a dancer uses to move or gesture. For example, a basic walk would change its aesthetic and emotional value as a dancer energized it into a run followed by several leaps. The basic movement is still a shift of weight from foot to foot. The difference is the amount of energy the dancer expends. Gestures, i.e., movements of any part of the body, are influenced similarly. In general gestures in dance are more stylized and less realistic: e.g., the extension of the hand and arm in greeting someone in dance may not look like "shaking hands" in everyday life.

Dance as art integrates the three elements. What the choreographer and dancers do with the basic dance elements will communicate the ideas, the emotions, and/or the aesthetics of the dance. Through the basic elements dance as performance art can stimulate audiences to cognitively, and especially, emotionally respond without ever using verbal stimuli. Dance for audiences is truly a right hemisphere experience.

Dance as Performance Art: Its Purposes

Dance as performance art has specific purposes: *narration, interpretation,* or *exploration.* Each places different requirements on the choreographer and dancers; each uses the basic dance elements in different ways. Audience expectations should adjust depending on the purpose of the dance.

Dance, as narrative tells a story, just like literature, or the performing arts of theatre, film, dramatic television and radio, and opera. Famous ballets like *The Nutcracker Suite* and *Swan Lake* exemplify dance telling a story.

In narrative dance plot, characters, relationships, and emotions will be revealed through physical action and the basic elements of dance. Therefore, what in everyday life is "I love you" may take two dancers several minutes to explore and communicate through dance. And, what the choreographer and dancer will reveal in the simple "I love you" are the emotional dimensions of the statement. The characters' feelings—naive young love, lust, romance, ecstacy, or gentle affection—will be expressed through the dancers bodies and movements.

All dance is interpretive. However, dance as interpretation means something specific. A choreographer might choose a specific activity (e.g., a rodeo), or event (e.g., a winter in Iowa), or literary work (e.g., Tennessee Williams' *A Streetcar Named Desire*), or musical work (e.g., music by Duke Ellington) and create an interpretation in dance of that activity, event, literary work, or musical work. The choreographer's vision is expressed by the skills of the dancers. As audience members we will not receive the "reality" of the rodeo, but its "essence" as captured in dance.

Dance can also exist in the purely aesthetic dimension of exploration. Choreographers and dancers may explore in performance the basic elements of time, space, and energy. This type of dance has no story or no specific source being interpreted. Exploratory dance is dance in its purest form. Audiences must respond specifically to the aesthetics of dance. Since there is no other referent, i.e., a story or a source, this purpose for dance may be the most difficult for audience members new to dance as a performing art to understand.

Knowing the purposes for dance as a performing art and the basic elements of dance give us a place to begin to build intelligent and knowledgeable reactions to a performance. Both the purposes and basic elements operate within the parameters of dance forms, the last informational key for dance audiences.

Forms of Dance

Theatrical dance may exist in a variety of dance forms. Since each form approaches the basic elements of dance in different ways, audience members need to know the basic distinguishing characteristics of theatrical dance forms. Armed with this last bit of information, then you will be ready to explore how to respond to the dance performance as it is happening to you.

Classical Ballet

Classical ballet is the most formal dance form that contemporary audiences may see regularly. Having originated many years ago in Italian masquerades and developed the royal courts of France during the 17th century, classical ballet possesses a long tradition and a defined "language," i.e., a code of physical movements and steps. Balletic terms in French reflect this tradition: e.g., *pas de deux*. The five classic ballet positions as they exist today have evolved from their roots centuries ago.

The regal, erect posture of the dancers distinguishes classical ballet. It has a strong verticality, which leads ballet to emphasize the line of the body as much as its movement in choreography. In watching classical ballet you feel that the dancers are lighter than the forces of gravity; they seem to defy gravity's pull. Only the feet of ballet dancers touch the floor. The rest of the body avoids the floor as a stimulus or an obstacle for expression, except in death scenes, e.g., in *Romeo and Juliet*, and *Swan Lake*. All of these characteristics can be illustrated by the ballerina dancing *en pointe*, i.e., on her toes. The verticality, the line, and the defiance of gravity complements the grace, beauty, and elegance in movements.

Beauty and elegance of movement are important qualities in classical ballet. The bending, stretching, extending, and balancing body movements of ballet are symmetrical and smooth. Since the curved arm and hand is thought more attractive, you see lots of curves in ballet. The tradition of the turned-out leg found in the classic positions is based in the presentation of the most attractive part of the leg—the calf and arched instep in extension. The dancers' skills should make the work of ballet look easy. Classical ballet dancers' movements as they leap through the air, dance on their toes, or move from side-to-side should appear effortless and ethereal. If that ease in performance is achieved, the dancers will have captured classical ballet's traditions and art.

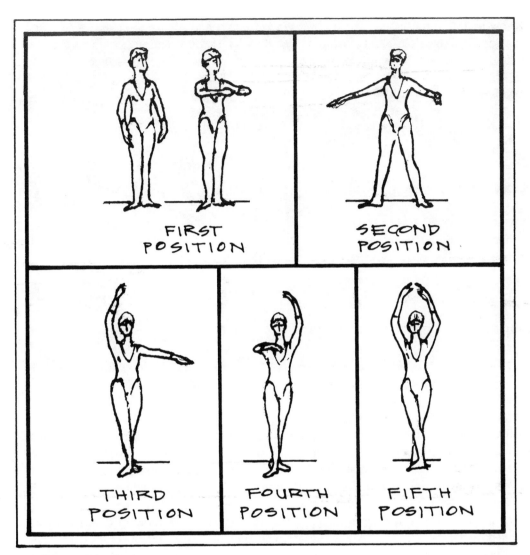

Five Classical Ballet Positions (Illustration by Fritz Szabo.)

Modern Dance

Modern dance has developed in the 20th century. At the turn of the century Isadora Duncan became its most well-known proponent. It started as a break with the traditions of the classical ballet form; dancers were freed to experiment. However, modern dance developed its own characteristics as influenced by its practitioners, e.g., Doris Humphrey, Charles Weidman, Martha Graham, Hanya Holm, and many others. At the end of the 20th century, modern dance has evolved varied approaches, which seem only limited by the imagination.

The Beethoven Quartet. The Oakland Ballet Company. (Courtesy of the Oakland Ballet Company.)

What are the characteristics of modern dance? In contrast to classical ballet which seems to defy gravity and the real world, modern dance gives into or resists gravity. The dancer's torso becomes very important. The body movements of modern dance may emphasize swinging and pulling in/pushing out movements, as well as the bending, stretching, extending, and balancing that we associate with ballet. The contraction and release of muscles in the torso beginning from the center of the body is a modern dance hallmark developed by Martha Graham. All of these movements distinguish themselves from ballet by allowing for asymmetry and for extensions of natural human movement. Finally, modern dance recognizes the floor as an integral part of choreography and dancing; modern dancers use the floor freely in falling, sitting, rolling, and lunging.

Jazz Dance

Jazz dance intends to surprise the audience. Its characteristics are usually high energy and excitement; a great flexibility in using the parts of the body; a reliance on a strong, underlying rhythms; and an isolation and syncopation of body parts integrated into the dance. All of these elements make for a dance form that is often overtly sexual.

Alvin Ailey American Dance Theatre in Alvin Ailey's *Revelations,* Photograph by Bill Hilton.

Isolation of body parts means that a dancer may highlight a movement by using only one body part while the rest of the body is still. For example, you might only move your pelvis while your shoulders and the rest of your body does not move. This directs focus to a single body part, and creates an element of surprise when viewed from the audience's perspective.

Other Dance Forms

Related to jazz dance is *tap dancing.* We have all seen this most popular form of theatrical dance. This American dance form combined African rhythms and Irish clog dancing to create a new form. Tap dancing emphasizes the feet and the sound that they make. Tap dancing surprises us with the sound made by the special shoes as well as by the dancer's movements. Our response to tap is aesthetic, a focus on the ability and technique of the dancer to excel.

111

Ethnic dance by the National Folk Ballet of Yugoslavia. (Courtesy of Columbia Artists Management.)

Ballroom dancing (another term for social dancing) is not usually seen in dance concerts. Occasionally, as in the case of the Broadway production of *Tango Argentina,* ballroom dancing is featured. Usually, the various kinds of ballroom dancing—waltz, fox trot, tango, rhumba, disco, jitter-bug, square dance—will appear as part of a musical theatre production.

Ethnic dance, i.e., the dances of cultures originally found outside of the United States, may receive theatrical performances. More often than not dance companies from other countries will present performances in the United States. In recent times ethnic dance companies visiting the United States included those from Scotland, Poland, China, Japan, Thailand, and Mexico.

Musical theatre dance (dances which occur within a structured musical comedy or musical play) requires a variety of dance forms. When watching dance in a musical, you may see jazz, tap, ballroom, modern, and maybe even ballet. Musical theatre choreographers must be adept in fashioning the dance to fit the music and the plot. Musical theatre dancers must possess the skill to perform in all the dance forms.

In musicals before 1943 or in operas or operettas, dance more often than not was used as an aesthetic diversion for the audience. 1943 was the real changing point for dance in musicals. Rodgers and Hammerstein's *Oklahoma* integrated dance into the action of the musical play. Agnes De Mille's choreography for the same production set new standards for excellence in musical theatre choreography. In a musical written after 1943 the dances are more likely to enhance the story of the musical, i.e., to advance the plot or reveal something about the characters, than just to provide an aesthetic dance entertainment.

Contemporary Trends in Dance

Although distinct historical and cultural roots for various dance forms exist, contemporary dance performances mix the forms of dance. It is not unusual to see theatrical dances merge ballet and modern dance techniques. Professional choreographers and dance companies have created new dances that are not strictly one form or the other, but that integrate elements of both in order to communicate ideas, designs, and feelings. New dance performances even include elements of jazz, or ballroom, or ethnic dance. Dance as performance art is reaching beyond the boundaries that define dance forms, and is using whatever form works for the choreography.

Audience Response to Dance

New-to-dance audiences sometimes feel that dance is the most difficult of performing arts to appreciate. Theatre is dramatic action, which we are familiar with on television and the movies. Music surrounds our lives in one form or another every day. Our familiarity with dance is from the "inside," i.e., we have socially danced. Much less familiar is the experience of sitting in a theatre and watching dance. As audience members we must develop approaches for becoming comfortable and knowledgeable in responding to dance from the "outside."

Why Do We Like Dance?

People like to "move to music." Even those who protest the loudest that they do not like to dance in public, in private love to "move to music." Dancing in public or in private is a popular social or individual activity. We like to dance because it makes us feel good. It is very difficult to maintain a bad mood when your body is reacting to an infectious bit of music. Our pleasure in social dancing comes from our emotional responses to the physical activity of dancing.

Although theatrical dance is more than moving to music, we can use our responses to social dancing as an approach to reacting with theatrical dance. Audiences have the abilities to empathize; empathy has been discussed as an important process in audience behavior. Just as we may flinch when a player gets tackled in a football game, so we can feel the exhilaration of a dancer leaping through space or the lighter than air quality of a ballerina on her toes. When we react with these physical actions, we are physically empathizing with the dancers. And, through physical reactions we are led to feel the dancers' emotions. We empathize with the dancers. This empathy will not be present in dance as exploration, where the aesthetic rather than the emotional dimension gets focus.

Our responses to theatrical dance are similar to the responses that we have when we actually dance, but we experience them vicariously through our abilities to "react with." And, with dance as performance art our emotional and physical responses are right hemisphere activities.

People like to have and to watch beautifully proportioned and skillfully trained human bodies. In fact we may dance for physical fitness. Numerous sports demand both. Part of the pleasure of watching gymnastics, synchronized swimming, and figure skating depends on the trained and conditioned human body. We respond to these sports aesthetically.

Theatrical dance gives us the aesthetic pleasure of watching superbly trained and conditioned human bodies. No matter what dance form, dance places rigorous physical and training demands on performers. Audiences like dance for this pleasure of seeing human beings move in ways that awe us. Dancers are human beings who can move like gods.

These responses to dance are "natural," in the sense that they are a part of our "nature" of being human: we like to move, and we like to watch trained, conditioned people move. However, theatrical dance is more than just moving to music. It is more than watching beautifully skilled performers. These natural responses are a beginning to a more learned and sensitive response to dance as a performing art.

Specific Methods to Enhance Your Response to Dance

Before attending a dance performance an audience member can take actions to enhance the experience. Since you may have little experience with theatrical dance, the more knowledge you have about the anticipated experience will prepare you cognitively for the performance. Reading about ballet, or watching video tapes of ballet gives you a better understanding about what may be a unfamiliar performance form. Watching a video especially provides a visual sense of what to expect, and an opportunity to "practice" responding to a dance performance. (Consult the television chapter for techniques for watching the performing arts on TV) During this preview of the performance utilize some of the following techniques to enhance theatrical dance reception.

Responding to the actual dance performance demands concentration on the present moment. Dance is very much an R-mode activity. You must help the right hemisphere to receive all the visual and aural stimuli that are part of a dance performance. All the skills of keeping yourself mentally in the present moment will assist you with dance. Choosing R-mode points of focus in the performance will keep the left brain from insisting on evaluating and analyzing while the performance is happening.

What are appropriate R-mode points of focus? The visual experience is primary. The dancers—both individually and in groups—are creating movements, patterns, and relationships that are pleasing or surprising to watch. The theatrical elements of design are also involved in dance performance. The costumes, lighting, and set design contribute to the performance's visual focus. By indulging your eyes in the visual sensations, reacting with the dance can begin to happen.

As you fill your eyes with the visual impact of dance, be sensitive secondarily to the music, and/or sounds which may accompany the performance. (Some theatrical dance is performed in silence.) The choreographer and the dancers have used this music or sound as an impulse for the creative work. Music/sound and dance are inextricably linked in the theatrical dance performance. By letting your aural senses to be filled with this potent accompaniment, your eyes may open to sensual aspects of the dance. Likewise, you may never listen to music as physically as you do when it is linked with dance.

Maximal R-mode reception of visual and aural stimuli demands specific present moment focuses, and a relaxed, comfortable attitude during the dance performance. To relax you must dismiss notions that dance will provide you with a content that you must sum up in a sentence. If choreographers and dancers wanted to do that, they would write articles and books. Dancers achieve their content through their "language" —the elements and forms of dance. Realizing that dance does not have to produce "meaning" should encourage a relaxed, comfortable acceptance of a performance. Remember: dance performance is not a mathematical equation; meaning in dance is not as concrete as 2+2=4.

As an audience member of theatrical dance performance, indulge your senses as a means to relaxation and comfort. Dance is a very sensual art. Indulging your senses of sight and hearing and touch (through physically reacting with) promotes relaxation. If your left-brain starts with its incessant questions (" What does this *mean?*" "I don't understand?" "Why are the dancers doing *that?*") , refocus your senses on the visual and aural stimuli without worrying about your need to understand every moment of what you are experiencing. Just relax (kick off your shoes if you can!) and indulge your senses. Your left-brain will get its chance after the performance is over.

After the performance is the time to reflect on the experience and ask yourself some questions that will lead to specific responses to dance as a performing art. Let's consider some of the questions that may deepen your perceptions of the dance performance.

The choreographer's contribution to the performance suggests several questions.

- Was the dance narrative, interpretive, or exploratory?
- What was the story?
- What event was interpreted?
- If dance elements were explored, how interesting were the choreographer's choices?
- How did the dance make you feel?
- Were your emotions engaged?
- Did the dance convey a meaning beyond feeling and movement?
- How creative were the choreographer's uses of space, time, and energy?
- Did the dance seem integrated, i.e., part of a whole?
- How did the theatrical elements of design influence the dance performance?
- Did the performers appear well-rehearsed?

These questions begin to explore your responses to the choreographer's contribution to the dance experience. They are all valid to ask and consider after the performance. Can you imagine trying to receive the stimuli of a theatrical dance performance and answering even one of the above questions? If you try, you miss the experience of the performance. For this reason we must restrain our left brain during the performance, and then let it loose after the performance to make sense of all the stimuli that we have received.

The dancers' contribution to the performance also encourages specific questions.

- How well did the dancers perform the movements?
- Were the movements performed with skill and any facility? (Can the dancers "do the steps?")
- What did the dancer communicate emotionally or cognitively?
- How well the dancers utilize space, time, and energy?
- Did the dancer's body suggest the conditioning and training needed to perform?
- Did the dancers interact well with each other at those moments when the choreography demanded it?
- Did any dancers provide you with moments of "magic," when you were awe-struck by their art?

After attending more and more dance performances, you may discover that the aesthetic specifics that these questions address will be integrated into your sensibilities. This integration is almost inevitable. It does not have to be a bad thing either. You will find that a performance that stimulated boredom and left-brain over-activity at your first dance concert will be understood in the present moment as a dancer who lacks proficiency or a choreographer who repeated the same movements too often. The integration of L and R mode thinking becomes a problem only if your left brain controls your responses in the performance's present moments.

Conclusion

Trust your senses and feelings first as you respond to theatrical dance. If the performance physically and emotionally engaged you so that you strongly reacted with it, the performance probably achieved its purpose. Do not worry about evaluating the performance as you experience it. If you concentrate on the present moment, you will recall a surprising amount of specific details as part of your response to the performance.

Dancers have an obligation to present performances that stimulate thoughts and/or emotions. Dance audiences have the responsibility to remain aware, alive, energized, and sensitive during the performance. Your eventual response will reflect the stimuli you received during the present moments of the performance combined with your knowledge of dance and your accumulated dance performance experience.

CHAPTER 7

Television, Film, Radio, and the Recording Arts

The performing arts of theatre, music, and dance have a long distinguished history, going back to the earliest periods of civilization. They also depend on the live audience, that special group which gathers to experience a live performance. As live performances they are truly interactive: artist and audience exchange feelings and thoughts at the same time in the same environment.

The performing arts of television, film, radio, and the recording arts are truly the "arts of the 20th century." They have resulted from technological advances that we associate with the last 100 years of scientific invention and development: electricity, electronics, computers, celluloid recording tapes, phonographs, miniaturized circuitry, sound and image transmission, satellite technology, photography, and laser technology. These performing arts have existed as significant contributors to art and entertainment for less than 100 years.

Television, film, radio, and the recording arts can be experienced to full satisfaction solitarily. And, although we often experience these 20th century arts in an audience, the experience that we have is not mutually interactive for performer and audience. Although we as audience members receive feelings and thoughts from the performers, the performers are not present to respond to the audience; no true exchange between performers and audience occurs. In this way, these performing arts may appear as passive media.

As passive media they encourage their audience toward a non-active acceptance of their product. Since there is no live performer and with television, radio, and the recording arts no "occasion," e.g., going to a movie theatre, to provide context for active listening, real connection with these media can be superficial or non-existent. Real "thinking" about these media often disappears. They are so omnipresent and pervasive in our lives that they become "background noise" rather than unique contributors to our sensibilities. Critics of

117

the performing arts may not take these media seriously; their audiences who know them so well often see no need to study them seriously.

The 20th century performing arts shape our thinking and perceiving of the world as strongly as the printing press and books did with our ancestors. In a technological society our thoughts and feelings are being shaped by images and sounds received from television, film, radio, and the recording arts. We decide Presidential elections on the visual images and "sound bites" of the candidates. We carry music everywhere we go with boom boxes and walkmen. We choose, consciously or unconsciously, clothing, perfumes, foods, and beverages derived from the fashions and styles promoted on the mass media. These pervasive media influence our thoughts and emotions daily.

Television, film, radio, and the recording arts even influence how we perceive the traditional performing arts of theatre, music, and dance. The mass media often determine our expectations and evaluative criteria for the traditional performing arts. As intelligent audiences for all performing arts we must understand the basic elements of these 20th century arts, and how we receive and process their special languages. Our study of these performing arts will also illustrate that at their best they stimulate us to "active" participation rather than merely "passive" acceptance. With this knowledge we may take steps to be more sensitive viewers and listeners.

Radio: Yesterday and Today

The magic of radio and its impact on our culture and society has diminished with the development of television. However, although the Golden Age of Radio has long past, radio is still an important part of our lives. It surrounds us in our homes and cars daily, if only as background for our daily activity. Hardly anyone says, "Oh, I'm going to sit down and listen to the radio."

People who lived in the 1930's, 1940's, and 1950's have different responses to radio than those in the TV generations. Radio was once the most popular entertainment medium in the United States. Programming for radio included all those staples that we associate with television today: children's programming, soap operas, comedy programs, mysteries, westerns, variety programs, drama, live musical programs, and news/current events. People actually stayed home to listen to their favorite radio program.

Where did radio come from? What was its influence in the past? What was the appeal of radio as a performance medium? What is its contemporary impact? What are its potentials for future development? Answers to all these questions will complete your understanding of radio as a performing art.

History of Radio

Radio began with experimenters trying to convert sounds into electromagnetic waves and to transmit them directly through space over a distance. As often happens what began as

Radio equipment in 1923. (Courtesy of the Department of Special Collections and University Archives, The Parks Library, Iowa State University.)

science was soon converted into practical applications. The scientists' successes and radio's conversion to entertainment uses occupied its beginning years of radio, 1906–1917.

Once radio became a reality, local stations developed to exploit its potentials. The period of 1918–1928 saw local radio programming emerge to serve the popular entertainment needs of listeners. Live music programs and a variety of news programs were most prevalent on local stations. The music programs featured singers, instrumentalists, and bands, always performing live and often before audiences. Radio was transmitting the live performing arts experience to thousands of people. During this start of radio programming little exploitation of the unique quality of radio performance was explored. Radio served merely as a transmitter of the performance over distance.

From 1929 to 1954 radio discovered its uniqueness as a performance medium. These years were known as the Golden Age of Radio. Local stations were merged into networks of stations. Three out of the four major radio networks are familiar to us today: ABC, CBS, and NBC. The fourth, MBS—the Mutual Broadcasting System—did not make the move to

Live local programming included bands. (Courtesy of the Department of Special Collections and University Archives, The Parks Library, Iowa State University.)

television in the 1950's. These four networks produced the same varied programming for radio each night and every week, as we know as part of our experience with television. Many of the "names" or programs recognizable from the early days of television were major radio performers or programs: Bob Hope, George Burns and Gracie Allen, Jack Benny, Bing Crosby, *The Lone Ranger, Gunsmoke,* and *Suspense.* Popular entertainment programs—soap opera, variety, comedy, mystery—joined with performing arts such as symphony orchestras, opera, and drama. And, most importantly, during this Golden Age producers, directors, and performers discovered the unique qualities of radio and developed them fully.

Television developed to its practical stage in the late 1940's, and began to move the radio out of the living room by the early 1950's. Radio programming on a national level did not die immediately; radio networks continued to produce daily and weekly programs. However, the direction for popular entertainment was apparent: 96 different half-hour radio programs played during the evening hours in the 1940's; by 1954 only 35 half-hour programs were playing weekly during radio's evening hours.

From 1955 to today, radio has evolved slowly into little more than a wireless juke box. Television won the battle to be the purveyor of popular entertainment. Network radio programming—except for news and sports—has disappeared. Radio has returned to the situation of its beginning years: local stations programming primarily music, news, and sports. Except this time the music programming is all recorded rather than live. Radio's unique qualities are ignored while it performs as just a transmitter of sounds.

Radio's Unique Qualities and Appeal

As a performing arts medium radio possesses two unique qualities: immediacy and the ability to stimulate our imaginations. Both qualities are similar to those received from the live performance arts—theatre, music, and dance. Radio achieves these qualities without an audience assembling in a theatre or auditorium, which makes the achievement more remarkable. Millions of people listening to radios feel the immediacy of the performers and the performance moment and have their imaginations stimulated to flights of fantasy.

The spatial distance between live performance transmitted by radio and the audience members does seem to reduce the immediacy of the performance. Listening to live radio broadcasts of music or variety programming still provides that special connection with the performers and performance. Contemporary examples of live radio programs prove that point.

Millions of opera lovers still tune in each Saturday for the broadcasts of the Metropolitan Opera that Texaco has sponsored and produced for years. The excitement of live opera performance, the responses of the audience at the Met reacting to the performance, the singers and orchestra performing in that exact same moment of receiving the music, all contribute to the immediacy of this radio broadcast. Also, the personalities of the announcer and of the people presenting the intermission features create a sense of personal connection that is renewed each time you listen to a broadcast.

Even more amazing than the continued success of the Met broadcasts was the contemporary success of Garrison Keillor's *A Prairie Home Companion.* This variety/talk program achieved significant radio audiences, long after the tradition of "listening to the radio" was dead. How could a variety program of singing, instrumental music, and storytelling on the radio achieve success in the contemporary era of visually exciting popular entertainment?

Keillor's success was based on a lot of factors. His program appealed to our desire to return to traditional values embodied in the family and small-town life. The stories of his fictional home-town, Lake Wobegon, Minnesota, touched the experiences of our lives and resonated with universal meanings. However, Keillor successfully utilized the immediacy of radio as a performing art. His voice, described as "molasses on a microphone," was so intimately personal that you felt he was sitting in your living room and talking to you over a cup of coffee. Garrison Keillor was alive with you every Saturday at 5 P.M. over Ameri-

121

can Public Radio! His program also gained immediacy by being performed before a live audience at the World Theatre in St. Paul, Minnesota. As a listener, you felt that you were there. Keillor knew how to use the immediacy and personal nature of radio as a performing art.

Radio also stimulates your imagination. As we listen to radio we create images in our minds of the people behind the voices and the action being suggested. This ability is especially crucial to dramatic programming, a type of programming that has been reduced since the demise of network radio. Recently, through the efforts of National Public Radio and independent producers, radio drama has received renewed attention. From 1973–1980 the Corporation for Public Broadcasting supported financially a major radio drama project called "Earplay." New and established writers created new plays for radio, which received the same professional quality of production as radio drama during the Golden Age of Radio. This project developed a small but loyal audience of radio drama listeners on NPR. In fact, many public broadcasting stations still air one to two hours of radio drama weekly.

What is the appeal of radio drama in our visual age of television, film, and video? Quite simply, it is the excitement of your imagination creating the visual pictures of the characters and action in your own minds. Our imaginations have the ability to create far more exciting situations than television or film. You do this daily as you daydream and fantasize. Radio drama provides a stimulus for this activity. Visualizations derived from our imaginations have the additional pleasure of being creations of our minds. Listening to radio drama is a truly creative activity.

Listening to radio drama demands a different kind of concentration and "willing suspension of disbelief" than experiencing drama on stage or in the visual media. Listening to a radio play is often very difficult; we simply are not used to *listen* to radios. Remember how they function as "wireless jukeboxes." However, even if we intensify our listening, we will hear different methods of communicating action and character than what we are used to in drama for theatre, television, or film. What are these differences?

Radio drama communicates plot, character, idea, mood, and dramatic action through dialogue, sound effects, and music only. Since radio drama has no opportunity to reinforce meaning through the visual image, these elements provide its essential foundation.

Dialogue must explain every action, environment, and character. To achieve these functions and yet to remain conversational and natural is very difficult. Therefore, you may hear lines like "Let me take your cup" or "The horse is distinctively light in color" or "Who's that standing in the door?" . What may at first sound like elementary or bad writing must be understood as necessary to assist our imaginations to see the action of taking the cup, to see the color of the horse in the distance, or to see the room with the person standing in the door. You will also notice that radio drama does not use the "long pause." Pauses on radio are simply "dead air," since no visual communication supports them.

Sound effects are in radio what scenery, costumes, and stage properties are in theatre, television, and film. Sound effects set the environment for dramatic action, create the illusion of distance, and/or clarify the action. Sound effects can be recorded, e.g., crickets chirping, sounds of a city street, or a car driving away; or they can be live, e.g., footsteps

Radio workshop students present a radio drama with all the paraphrenalia needed to create the reality of the drama. (Courtesy of the Department of Special Collections and University Archives, The Parks Library, Iowa State University.)

approaching a door, the door opening, galloping horses. Sound does not just support the creation of environment and action as it does in theatre, film, and television, but actually creates the environment and action in our imaginations.

Music has two general purposes in radio drama: 1) as a bridge or interlude between scenes to suggest the passage of time and/or a change of place; and 2) as a creator or reinforcer of the mood of the dramatic action. In this second respect, music in radio drama functions similarly to the musical underscoring with which we are so familiar with in television and film. The first purpose is unique to radio drama. As a ''radio drama convention,'' we must accept it to understand the flow of a radio drama. After a musical bridge in a radio drama, the audience must be especially listening to the dialogue and sound effects which define the new time or place more precisely.

Radio as a performing art possesses immediacy and the ability to stimulate your imagination. Radio may still work its effects on you in this time of visual entertainment, if you concentrate on listening and practice listening to radio drama. The reward of heightening your perceptions and sensibilities make listening to radio drama as a performing art most pleasurable.

Film: Dramatic Art in a Visual Language

Like all the performing arts, film communicates thoughts and feelings to an audience. However, film as performance art is uniquely a visual dramatic art. Films primarily exist for an audience as series of images. Although music, sound effects, and dialogue add to a film's impact, the story of a dramatic film is told primarily through images.

At first film appears very similar to the theatre since many elements appear in both: actors, design, drama, and directors. Closer observation clarifies the salient differences between film and theatre. Understanding these differences will help your enjoyment of both theatre and film.

Contrasts Between Theatre and Film

Both theatre and film have a foundation in drama. However, drama in the theatre is conceived initially in words; perusing any play will show the words of the dialogue carrying the dramatic action. Because of this initial conception in words, theatrical productions tend to follow a logical sequence: C follows B follows A. Although some experiments in drama have departed from the logical sequence of events and flashbacks and flashforwards are used in stage drama, most theatre follows this linear pattern in the arrangement of the events of the drama. Film is initially conceived in visual terms. Film scripts describe the visual action; dialogue carries only part of a film's dramatic action. Visual language gives film greater freedom in ordering dramatic action. Moving images may have an impact on our perceptions in a random fashion, as in a dream. These images may be free of any inner logic.

Film is based on images; theatre is based on words. You can attend a theatrical performance, close your eyes, and still receive through the dialogue the basic ideas and emotions of the drama. If you close your eyes while watching a film, you soon discover that you cannot follow the dramatic action. The film depends not on dialogue but on images to tell its story.

Images versus the live performers define another difference between theatre and film. The theatre experience brings together the event (the production), the audience, and the actors. The film experience does not. The event was filmed months or years before the audience experiences it. And, quite obviously, as audience members we respond to images not live actors. Film over the years has developed techniques in cinematography and special effects that give film almost the same immediacy as theatre.

The moving image on a screen has been the hallmark of film as an art form since its inception in the 1890's. Although the early history of the motion picture emphasized a linear narrative structure, a fixed camera which only captures movement in the plane of the screen, and theatrical scenery, film fascinated its early audiences with visual action. From unstructured bits of action in the earliest film to the long scenes of linear narrative the moving images held audiences enthralled. In fact some of the feature length silent films illustrate the story-telling ability of visual language in its purest form; no sound or "talk" interferes with the direct impact of the image.

With the arrival of the "talkies" in 1927 (*The Jazz Singer* was the first "talking" film) film reverted to the static form of the earliest silents. Just as visual action on a screen fascinated film audiences during film's early history, audiences now were amazed at how films could talk. However, film art has evolved full-circle; now in its story-telling film has returned to using its full visual potential.

Finally, the most noticeable difference between theatre and film is point of view. We watch a play as *we* want to watch it. As we sit in the theatre, we focus our senses on whatever we wish. The theatre director will try to guide our focus through the actors' and designers' arts. However, the audience ultimately has the control to look at, to listen, and to respond to anything on stage. We watch a film as the *filmmaker* wants us to see it. As we sit in the film theatre, we focus only on what the director/filmmaker wishes. If the director wants us to look at a character's right eye, we will have no choice, even though we might wish to look at the character's whole body or even at another character. The filmmaker controls the point of view in film; the audience controls the point of view in the theatre.

How Film Communicates to an Audience

Although film communicates through visual, verbal, and aural stimuli, visual language is primary. Audiences discover character behavior and understand the dramatic action through the images of a film. Understanding how the filmmaker uses the camera to communicate is important to film appreciation. Likewise editing, music, and special effects contribute to the communication process in filmmaking.

Film scripts and stage plays pursue the same goals. They both attempt to select events to tell a story which will develop believable characters and reveal human conduct. These stories will usually have a central theme or idea. The difference is that the film script will emphasize visual language while the stage play gives focus to dialogue, to verbal language.

The Camera and Visual Language

The cameras are the film directors' "eyes." The camera's eyes determine the audience's response. Film directors use cameras to create an illusion of depth by providing a variety of angles of vision, and to encourage an emotional or cognitive response from the audience.

Film is a two dimensional art. The camera views an object with one eye; that image is eventually projected on a two dimensional screen. A fixed camera provides no depth of

Long shot from GONE WITH THE WIND. (Courtesy Ted Turner Enterprises. Copyright © 1939 Selznick International Pictures, Inc. Ren. 1967 Metro-Goldwyn-Mayer Inc. Photo from the Wisconsin Center for Film and Theater Research.)

vision. Viewing early silent film illustrates the flat, two dimensional nature of film shot by a fixed camera. Yet, when we watch film today, we seldom are aware of its two dimensional nature. In fact we probably feel that film has all the qualities of ''real life.''

The filmmakers solved this early problem of lack of depth in film by creating an illusion of depth through a variety of angles of vision. The film director chooses from a variety of camera shots to create this illusion: 1) a stationary camera with a changing lens; 2) a moving camera; 3) moving performers; or 4) a combination of all the above choices.

Cameras may remain stationary, i.e., the camera does not move, with only the lens changing to create different shots. Various familiar shots use this approach. For example, a *long shot* might establish two characters seated in an empty movie theatre; a *medium shot* might follow showing a seated man and woman from the waist up staring at the flickering movie screen; a *close-up* on the man's face shows his eyes moving to look at the woman. If the camera smoothly moves from long to medium to close-up, or in the opposite direction

Medium shot from THE WIZARD OF OZ (Courtesy of Ted Turner Enterprises. Copyright © 1939 Loew's Inc. Ren. 1966 Metro-Goldwyn-Mayer, Inc. Photograph from the Wisconsin Center for Film and Theater Research.)

from close-up to medium to long, the camera is equipped with the technical apparatus to do zoom shots. Within the medium or long shot the director can direct the audience's attention by focusing sharply on the figures in the foreground or on those in the background. Throughout any film the director uses patterns of long, medium, close-up, and zoom shots to create the illusion of depth, and the images to tell the story.

Illusions of depth also may be created by moving the camera. Two types of moving camera shots exist for the director. When the base of the camera remains stationary, but the camera itself moves, the shots are called the pan (the camera turns right or left) and the *tilt*. When the entire apparatus, camera and base, moves, a greater variety of shots is created: the *dolly* shot (the camera moves toward or away from the performer), the *truck* shot (the camera moves right or left), the *boom* shot (camera is attached to a crane which moves), and the *travel* shot (a portable camera is moved by a person, by a car or plane, or by a mechanical tracking apparatus).

Finally, moving the actor enhances illusions of depth. This method is not used as much as creating a variety of camera shots. In fact, film actors move considerably less than their counterparts in the theatre. However, when actors move in concert with the changes in camera shots, the audience receives a believable illusion of depth.

Camera shots also communicate emotionally and cognitively to an audience. The director's decision to shoot a long-shot rather than a close-up, or to use a travel shot rather than a stationary shot affects your response to that image. Empathy occurs more easily when the camera is close-up; the audience must look at the person dealing with the emotion. Long shots establish quickly the environment for the action. Looking up at a character gives you a sense of weakness or vulnerability; looking down at a character gives you a sense of strength or power. Zooming in on dramatic action is surprising and exciting. When these camera shots are combined with editing, music, and special effects, the filmmaker's influence over the audience becomes all the more powerful.

Film Editing, Music, and Special Effects

Film editing is the process of taking all the raw footage that has been shot and arranging it into a meaningful whole. The film editor decides when to cut from one image to another, when to dissolve or fade from images, and when to superimpose one image over another. During editing entire sections of the film may be discarded. The editing process decides the look of the final product. Because of the importance of film editing, film directors work closely with editors in determining the final cut of the film, or edit the film themselves. Editing solidifies the director's control over the audience.

Through the editing process the director maintains control over the audience's perceptions of tempos, moods, and dramatic action. Quick cuts build the tempo and mood of a chase sequence or of a murderer pursuing a victim. Dissolves and fades support the romantic mood of a first kiss. Editing creates the horror of the murderer entering the front door and proceeding upstairs to the bedroom, while the victim awakes, thinks she hears something, and rises in bed listening. Editing allows the film director, in contrast to the stage director, to be assured that the final product seen by the audience is aesthetically correct.

Musical underscoring helps the director guide audience's emotions. Imagine the lack of tension and excitement in the opening sequences of *Jaws* without the music supporting the ripples in the water and the unseen shark getting closer and closer to the person in the water. Musical underscoring, which supports the director's ideas, is the last major element added before the final cut of the film is released.

After the film has been edited, the director and the composer sit down to watch the final edited version. The director talks about where music is needed and the quality of the required music. The composer then completes the score, orchestrates it, and arranges for the musicians to record it. The score corresponds absolutely with the action of the film. The music track is laid down in absolute synchronization with the film and the sound track. In fact, the film is screened as the musicians play the music to assure absolute synchronization. The film score supports the director's ideas and the control exerted over the audience's perceptions.

Audiences know the power of special effects in filmmaking. Whether the effect is a space ship racing through galaxies in the 22nd century, a miniature human being whisking through the blood stream of a human body, a flood of water rushing through a cave, or a man being transformed into a fly, special effects dazzle and entertain the film audience. They also allow the director to tell the story; they emotionally engage us and increase our connection with the film. Their purposes go beyond dazzling us. Special effects provide the director with unlimited ways to communicate with the audience. Special effects allow film to explore imaginatively worlds that the physical reality of the stage excludes for theatre.

Why Are Audiences Drawn to Film?

Films as popular entertainment are an escape from the everyday world. We can lose ourselves in fantasy worlds or in reality adventures that turn out happily. Escape is a major reason why audiences still flock to the movies in spite of the omnipresence of television and video cassettes. Film, however, attracts audiences with other satisfactions.

Audiences love good stories. Human beings love to watch imitations of action. Aristotle's "mimesis" continues to be compelling in the art of film. Film like the novel can tell long stories with a wealth of detail; neither theatre or television can do this as well. These complex stories of films—being able to leap in time and place, and to introduce generations of characters—makes movie attendance as compelling as a good "read" of the latest novel. And, of course, film brings the characters to life before your eyes. The successes of best-selling novels, like *Gone With the Wind*, when transferred to film testify to our love of a good story.

Film satisfies audiences because as an art it is involving, like the theatre. In the theatre the performance of the live actors—always slightly larger than life—create an immediacy that a recorded art like film cannot match. With film the viewing environment contributes significantly to the ease with which we involve ourselves in the dramatic lives of characters.

The large film screen replaces the larger than life performances of live actors in the theatre. The projected images are huge and all encompassing to our vision. They draw us into the action on the screen. Contrast our involvement with the images on the film screen with our detachment with the images on the television screen. The TV screen is smaller than life; the action, no matter how compelling, seems diminished by the size of the TV screen. Empathic involvement with television drama demands intense concentration on the audience's part.

The film theatre like the theatre experience increases the opportunity for involvement by turning off the lights. Since you are less aware of immediate environment, including even the person sitting next to you, you are more inclined to engage yourself in the immediacy of the film. Dimming the lights really is not needed to see a film. Darkness satisfies our desire for aloneness as we involve ourselves in the film experience.

Films fulfill our needs for escape, for good stories, and for an opportunity to become emotionally and cognitively engaged in a dramatic experience. As we become more familiar with the great variety of experience available in films and acquire more knowledge about film as a performance art, we grow to appreciate film not only for its action adventures but also for how it can reveal the nature and meaning of human behavior.

How to Respond to a Film

Because our experience with film is extensive, we may know how to watch and to respond to movies. Our viewing experience has provided us with many skills in interpreting and understanding visual language. By adding knowledge from your study of the medium, you will only enhance your present abilities to watch and respond to film. Knowledge of the art is the first step—as with all the performing arts—to informed critical response.

Increasing awareness of film's language must be complemented by a commitment to active engagement with the film at the time of experiencing it. Let the film access your right brain's thinking processes. Give the film the opportunity to impact on you as the filmmaker wishes. Avoid left brain analysis of story, acting, or technical matters. Know that you will give your analytical powers their chance after the film is over. If you allow the film your total concentration, you will have been "actively" involved in the experience. You will have avoided the detached, objective, evaluative, and often passive acceptance of film art.

After the film evaluate the experience. Because you have concentrated fully on receiving all the stimuli, as the director planned and controlled them, you will find your response—either positive, neutral, or negative—will be specific and detailed. Your strongest response will be emotional. Your emotions will have been involved in the film. Try to explain your feelings in specific terms relating to the film experience. What was the film saying about human behavior, relationships, or society? Do you agree with the filmmaker's perspective? Then, the aesthetic analysis looks at the acting, directing, and design elements. How did the aesthetic elements influence your emotional and cognitive responses to the film? At this point your knowledge of the camera, editing, musical underscoring, special effects, plus your accumulated knowledge of theatrical elements of acting and design comes into play. Responses to films have much to draw upon.

Finally, don't be disappointed that you can not remember everything about the film. Like any art repetition of the experience will provide greater insights. Since film is a recorded art, you can return and view the film again; like the literary arts, the recorded arts allow this repeated experiencing. Watching a film for a second or third time will stimulate you to concentrate on different aspects than during your first viewing. You now know the story and its emotional impact. You may find yourself concentrating on aesthetic considerations: camera work, editing, lighting, images, visual symbols, music, acting, costumes, decor. In fact second and third screenings of favorite films are wonderful ways to experience the aesthetic and technical elements of film. Take advantage of film as a recorded art to learn and develop your appreciation of film's aesthetics.

As we move toward the 21st century, film will increase in its abilities to entertain and to engage audiences. Its potential as a performing art is truly awesome. However, to achieve its potential film needs audiences who are more than just passive receptors of escape entertainment.

Television: The Omnipresent Performing Art

We take for granted television's presence in our lives and its influence on our perceptions of all the performing arts. Our earliest memories include television as a part of our lives. Our earliest attempts to "stay up late" related to watching late night television. We developed early our favorite programming, and scheduled our study and play time around those programs. Our attention spans for sustained focus on dramatic programs have been influenced by TV's 8–1 2 minute performance segments, which are dictated by the need for commercials.

Since television is so familiar and commonplace, we take its presence in our lives for granted. There is nothing "special" in sitting down to watch a television special anymore. Since we know television so well, we may not consider it seriously as a performing art. We may even feel that we already know everything about viewing and evaluating television.

Our basic response to television is passive. Like radio we often have television "on," but are not really viewing it. It provides background noise, or amusement when a program catches our interest or attention. And, if we are actually watching it, we often remain detached from the present moment of experiencing. Our left brain comments on, ridicules, or evaluates the TV program, thereby blocking the aesthetic experience. We may use the TV program as a stimulus for the ongoing and constant conversation among the TV viewers. Active participation, as has been defined throughout this book, may not be a part of our audience response to television.

Television as a performing art needs commitment of your attention in the present moment. Before exploring ways to experience television performance, the unique qualities of "audience" as it relates to television need to be fully understood. Possessing those understandings will provide the solid foundations for responding to TV as performance art.

Television and Audience

The Individual Viewing Experience

The individual audience member for television receives a performance in a much different way than the audience member for film or theatre. Television viewing is not necessarily a group experience; much TV watching occurs alone. Watching television does not demand going to a special environment like a theatre; television viewing happens in your home. Because television viewing is not an "occasion," the viewer is more likely to passively receive the presentation rather than be actively engaged.

The television audience member responds to television in the same ways as listening to radio, even though watching dramatic performances seems more similar to the film or theatre experience. Theatre audiences actively feed back to the live actors; film audiences feed back similarly, even though they are responding to recorded images on a screen. Television audiences have little of the group audience feedback behavior, e.g., applauding, laughing. The solitary person or the very small group viewing in their homes feel no compulsion to respond actively to the performers. Active audience engagement is not impossible, only rare. The viewing environment and the medium itself work against engagement.

We watch television in familiar surroundings, which are fairly well lighted and not immune to the distractions of everyday life. Telephones ring; family members or friends come and go throughout the TV performance; pets demand attention; and people with whom we are watching demand attention. In fact, we have learned how to do other activities *while* watching television: cooking, laundry, eating, homework, housework, playing games, reading, conversing, and many other activities. For all of these reasons, the television audience member has a detached involvement with the experience.

The television medium also encourages detachment. The television screen is small when compared with the film screen or the stage of a theatre. With television we watch characters and action that are *smaller than life,* smaller than life action that is recorded. These qualities work against engagement. The new large television screens encourage more involvement, but our TV viewing behavior and environment work against the type of willing suspension of disbelief and empathy encountered in the theatre and with film.

Although the experience for the television audience member differs from the film and theatre audience member, television remains the most popular of the performing arts. The average American spends over 40 hours per week watching TV; with cable the average goes higher. According to Gallup polls 33% of us say watching television was the most enjoyed way of spending an evening. More people are watching more television than ever before, with 90.4 million households with television sets.

The Audience and Television Programming

The concept of ''the audience'', i.e., a *single* group of people watching television, really does not exist. The television programmers and producers must appeal to *many* audiences. These audiences may be classified by age, sex, occupation, income, or education. Tracking the compositions of audiences for television programming is crucial to this popular entertainment mass medium.

Demography describes the characteristics of any audience as well as its size. Demography is the study of characteristics of human populations. Television networks hire research organizations, like the A.C. Nielsen Company, to provide them with the demographic data about their programming. Within the television business these research organizations are known as ''ratings services.''

The method of tracking television audiences depends on the use of a ''people meter.'' A small sample of the United States population (approximately 4000 households) participate. All the television sets in the household are electronically monitored; they report to a computer which programs are being watched. Someone watching is asked to push buttons on an electronic device that provides information about "who is watching." The ages and sex of the viewers are the most important data for the ratings service. The "people meter" provides the networks detailed information about the audience on a daily basis. A.C. Neilsen is developing a "passive people meter," which will consist of a camera-like device and a computer. This image recognition system would identify household members and record their behavior every second they watch television. The passive system will give even greater accuracy to television demography.

The demography of the television audience serves two important purposes for television networks and their programmers. For any given time A.C. Nielsen can provide the percentage of the audience which is watching a particular program. Being first at a given hour allows the network to charge significantly more for the cost of a commercial minute. In the mid-1980's *The Cosby Show* on NBC went head-to-head with the first half hour of *Magnum, P.I.* on CBS. *The Cosby Show* was the number one television program in the United States at that time. For that half-hour, NBC could charge $270,000 for a 30 second commercial, while CBS's 30 second commercial rate was $110,000. The "ratings game" and the information provided by demographics allowed for this differentiation. Demography directly affects the income of networks and the "life" of any television program.

Demographic data also gives the networks an audience profile, i.e., a description of the typical viewer. This information sells specific programming to commercial sponsors. Advertisers usually have "target audiences" for their products. For example, advertisers looking for teenagers may buy time on a specific program if the demographic data indicate a significant teenager audience. The two top demographic groups to advertisers are women 18–4 9 and men 18–4 9. A show that succeeds with either group will survive with the network even if its overall rating is low.

The relationship of "the audience" to television programming is very business-like. The chief consideration for programming is getting the public to accept it. Programming is the *only* product offered for sale by the TV networks. You may hear talk of selling "time," but sponsors will not purchase "time" unless it is surrounded by interesting programming.

Who controls television programming? The networks? The producers of programs? The advertisers? No. The audience—or should we say audiences—controls programming. Television is a business; the product is programming. The program that the largest portion of the audience chooses to watch receives favor—with networks, producers, and advertisers. This causes the "clone" approach to TV programming. When a specific program, e.g., *The Cosby Show,* becomes enormously successful, other producers and networks create similar types of programs hoping for the same success. Audiences control programming for the mass medium of television.

This audience control produces more popular entertainment than art. Since the creators of television programming are driven by what the market wants, they have little opportunity to examine those ideas and issues that may disturb the mass audience. We desire popular entertainment performances that are easy to relate to (simple plots, characters, action) and comfortable to experience (no challenging of status quo beliefs or ideas). Since art pushes the audience toward challenging the status quo and serious consideration of ideas and issues, television provides fewer opportunities to do this than the other performing arts. The marketplace and the mass audience indirectly exert creative control over the television product.

TV Audiences Then And Now

The history of television illustrates another way to understand the concept of the audience as it relates to TV. Television began like radio in the hands of the experimenters in the 1930's and 1940's. During the 1930's ordinary people were amazed by demonstrations of this technological marvel that could transmit sound and pictures from one location to another. By the time that technology allowed for the transmission of image and sound through the air so that local stations developed, manufacturers had television sets ready to receive those signals. Networks brought together these independent local stations. The television industry was ready to grow.

The first television programs were live, just like theatre performances except they were transmitted by electrical impulses to the locations where they were viewed. The early programs gathered audiences in television studios to respond to the performances. Performing for live studio audiences created an immediacy very similar to that achieved in the theatre. Watching such a program in your home was similarly exciting and engaging.

As television developed as a performance medium, several changes reduced the immediacy of television programming. Technology developed so that programs could be filmed or recorded on video tape. This allowed producers to avoid the hassles associated with live television production. Concurrently, studio audiences became less evident except for game shows and variety shows. When audience responses were needed, taped reactions were used; for situation comedy programs the "laugh track" became a staple of TV production. Although the elimination of "live" production and audiences gave producers greater flexibility and artistic freedom, the immediacy of watching television was greatly reduced. Watching TV became less of an "event" and more of a routine.

In the 1970's and '80's the audience returned to television programming. Situation comedies dumped the "laugh track" and performed the show live in front of a studio audience. Once again the laughter complemented the specific actions on the program. Even though the program was recorded (" recorded live before a studio audience"), its chances to engage the home audience was greater. The home audience responded as an extension of the studio audience; they felt a part of the dramatic or comedic experience.

Live audiences have become even more integrated into television programming formats. Talk programming, e.g., Phil Donahue, Geraldo Rivera, Oprah Winfrey, Morton Downey, specifically involves the studio audience in the action of the program. "The whole event is altered by their presence and inclusion," says Phil Donahue. Audience members "create an adrenaline and energy level" which affect both host and guests. This involvement positively engages the audience watching at home.

134

Television in the 1950's emphasized local programming just like radio's beginnings. "The Magic Window" with Betty Lou MacVay on WOI-TV, Ames/Des Moines, IA. (Courtesy of the Department of Special Collections and University Archives,. The Parks Library, Iowa State University.)

Television has come full circle in realizing the power of the live studio audience to energize and enliven programs. We have called this energy "immediacy" in our discussion of the performing arts. Even more immediacy could be created if more live television performance were presented. The annual presentations for the Emmy, Grammy, Oscar, and Tony awards illustrate immediacy and the creation of a special event that is the potential of live television.

Trends Affecting Television Viewing

"Grazing" As a Television Viewing Phenomenon

Television has encouraged a shortened attention span in viewers because of the commercials which interrupt programming in 8 to 10 minute intervals. However, studies by the Communication Technology Laboratory at Michigan State University and by Frank N.

135

Magid Associates (as reported in *Channels* magazine) suggest a greater restlessness in viewers in selecting programs. Technology has permitted viewers to become "grazers".

"Grazing" is the process of watching several television programs at one time, of moving through the channels, of pausing for short intervals with certain programs, and then of moving on again as the program becomes less interesting. The developments of remote control devices and cable television make grazing possible. Since 75% of TV households have remote control and more than 50% have cable television, the impact of this practice on television programmers and advertisers is changing the realities of the business.

The Michigan State study of 800 5th and 10th grade students showed that "grazing" occurred as the program became less interested, or in between MTV segments, or at other logical points in the programming breaks, e.g., commercials. The Magid survey shows more than half of the viewers between 18 and 34 regularly watch more than one TV show at once; a smaller number of the same demographic group watch three or more shows at once. Men tend to graze more than women. The Magid study describes the viewing audience as "restive, fickle, quick to judge, alternately demanding or preoccupied, hard to please, even harder to hold onto." The possibility exists that watching television—not watching TV programs—has become a form of entertainment itself.

These studies point to the audience's dissatisfaction with TV programming. If the programs are compelling and engaging the viewer, the impulse to graze would not occur. The grazing phenomenon supports several contemporary studies showing that viewers were not happy with television. The studies also illustrate the continued shortening of the attention of television audiences. Audiences have less patience with programming; if the program does not interest the viewer in the first few minutes, the viewer begins to graze. Of course, the shortening attention space has residual impact on all the performing arts, when the TV trained audience member faces a dance concert, symphony, play, or film.

Increasing Appetite for the Visually Exciting

Studies and ratings have shown that more viewers are responding favorably to TV programming that emphasizes the visual and diminishes plot and characterization. The production values of music videos, which create impressions through a rapid montage of sound and image, have been felt in the traditional productions of television dramatic programming.

The success in the 1980's of "Miami Vice," notable for its look and sound rather than for a coherent story line, testifies to the audience's demand for the visual. Rather than using traditional story-telling techniques, "Miami Vice" built the dramatic action by using visual imagery, rock music, and quick cut editing methods. Aristotle might say that the element of drama called "spectacle" was receiving emphasis at the expense of plot and character. External action got focus; internal action of characters and ideas was diminished.

What is the importance of these trends to us as audience members of all the performing arts? Today's audiences must be flexible in order to adapt to the performing arts. Knowledge of television's effects on our attention spans and our performance expectations allows us to adjust when we face music, dance, theatre, or film. Failure to adjust may lead to unsatisfying performance experiences based on the very narrow perceptions that prolonged television viewing can develop.

How to Respond to Television as a Performing Art

Responding to television as a performing art is more difficult in some ways than responding to dance, music, theatre, and film. All four of those performing arts exist in environments which encourage maximal reception of the art. Also, our reception of those four performing arts are consciously controllable to some degree. In contrast, television occurs in our homes, which normally are not associated with receiving a performing art and usually do not maximize reception elements, e.g., special seating and lighting. Television, as a routine part of our daily existence, invites a more uncontrolled response in the present moment; our response is based on our TV behavior developed over years of watching it.

We often joke about the "couch potato," the person who sits for hours in the same place mesmerized by the TV screen and accepting all programming passively, i.e., never actively engaging his/her senses, emotions, or thoughts in evaluating or understanding what they are watching. Passive "watching" becomes the major activity. Television has an almost hypnotic power to bind us to our seats, even when we recognize how unsatisfactory the programs are. How can we avoid the "couch potato" phenomenon when we choose to experience television as a performing art?

The same techniques that were suggested for the other performing arts, especially theatre and film, apply to receiving the television experience. All the techniques of engaging the right hemisphere, of allowing the experience to "wash over" you like a wave, and of postponing left hemisphere evaluation and analysis apply to being an active member of the television audience. You should be aware that sustaining these practices with television will be more difficult due to your developed practices of TV watching.

Active television watching demands conscious attention-giving and focus on the experience. The environment and your past practices will push you toward the easy, passive "couch potato" responses. Resist their draw! If possible take control of your environment. Lower the lighting as theatres do. Sit in a different seat or with a different posture to remind you of your desire for active participation. Try sitting closer to the television set to increase your perception of the size of the screen. Ask fellow viewers not to talk during the program. If audience "noise" is not controllable, practice your new approach to TV watching alone; you will be surprised how much you can improve your concentration on television experiences through solitary viewing.

Most importantly: concentrate on the stimuli from the program that are bombarding your senses. Television uses the same visual language of film—different types of camera shots, editing, music, sound effects. Television controls your perceptions of the reality by showing you only what the director wants you to see. These active techniques help you become a more engaged and receptive viewer of television as a performing art.

Conclusion

As opposed to the performing arts that you have little experience with, television challenges you to break old habits and routines in order to explore it as a performance art. We grow up learning to be passive receptors, "couch potatoes," and disassociated listeners to television. If we have been really alienated by television programming, we may reject it totally as a choice among the performing arts.

You may renew or reactivate your reception and perception of television by treating it as an active audience experience. Conscious focus on receiving the sensual stimuli combined with conscious efforts to modify environmental and personal factors will open television to you as a performing art. The world of television—its strengths, its potentials, and its weaknesses—will come alive like a new medium, or at least like the medium that burst on the country's sensibilities in the late 1940's and '50's.

The results of changes in your viewing habits will make you a more knowledgeable and perceptive watcher of TV, and will heighten your critical evaluation of programming. And, with these changes, you will have no fear of living your life as a "couch potato."

The Recording Arts and Audiences

The recording arts are a relatively new addition to the performing arts. Because of phonograph recordings, cassettes, and compact discs (CD's), we are now able to listen to musical performances in our homes, in our cars, and even walking down the street. Dance and theatre performances may be recorded on video tape; we may perform the recording task ourselves with our video cassette recorders (VCR's). Video tapes of our favorite contemporary or classic films are available for rental or purchase. This explosion of recording arts has had a great impact on us as audiences.

The recording arts have given performing arts' audiences the opportunity usually reserved for the literary and visual arts. The live performing arts are ephemeral, i.e., they exist in time. Film, although it is recorded, has the required needs of a large screen and a theatre in order to receive the art in the manner the filmmaker intended. The recording arts are fixed-in-time like literature, paintings, sculpture, and architecture. This opportunity allows us to return over and over to experience a particular piece of music, or a play, or a film. As we respond, we can stop the music or video, rewind, and receive the same visual or aural stimuli as we had just experienced. The recording arts have fixed certain performing arts in time, giving audiences increased chances to study and explore the aesthetic achievements of these arts.

Impact on Audiences

The ability to reexperience performances not only allows you to increase your understanding and appreciation of a specific performance, but also gives you opportunities to

138

practice your audience listening skills. The suggestions about how to respond to theatre, dance, music, television and film can now be tried in the privacy of your home and without committing lots of money for tickets. Audiences may "rehearse" their involvements with the performance experience; up to now your rehearsal required a theatre or a concert hall. Now with the recording arts your preparation for a performance may proceed whenever you have the time.

Preparation for a live performance might preview an unknown piece of music before hearing a concert, or a ballet or opera before seeing it. This preview rather than diminishing the live performance will enhance it; you will be more comfortable in the theatre because you have a familiarity with the music, ballet, or opera. You could do the same with a Shakespearean play that you plan to attend. Excellent videos of Shakespeare's plays exist, and will make you familiar with the plots and characters as well as making his language more easy to listen to and understand. Although you could not "preview" a current film on video before seeing it at your local theatre, you could prepare yourself for the visual experience by looking at film videos by the same director, actors, or writer. This could expand your knowledge of the backgrounds of the creative artists involved in the film.

The recording arts also increase the audience's flexibilities in seeking out performance arts. Before the recording arts we had to wait for the arrival in our town of specific films, or wait until the local live theatres produced a particular play, or travel to larger towns to see a ballet or opera of our choice. The recording arts provide the opportunities of seeing and hearing arts whenever we want. Our time with the arts may be efficiently as well as aesthetically used.

Realistic Expectations for the Recording Arts

Obviously the recording arts are unique, and not merely replications of the live performing arts and film. When we sit down to enjoy recorded arts, important awarenesses about their unique qualities when contrasted with the other performing arts will give us realistic expectations. Just as we must adjust our receptors and use our knowledge as we face each performing art, we must do the same with the recording arts. And, since our normal behavior may ignore these distinctions, they need our attention.

One performing art transfers completely and truthfully to video recording. Any television program conceived for the medium will communicate with all its aesthetic values intact when recorded on a VCR. If the program was originally a feature film, then you will face the same problems of watching a film on video.

Music transfers magically to records, cassettes, and CD's. In fact you may be able to hear a musical performance with greater fidelity and acoustical perfection than you can hear in some concert halls. Technology has served music well. The immediacy of the live performance—you and the performers existing in the space performance space—is lost. However, record producers can even provide some of that excitement by recording live performances. Good concert recordings capture much of the tension of live performance, the interactive feedback of performer and audience, and the audience's responses. Audiences of recordings need to know that some recordings could never be reproduced in a live performance. Because technology can tape numerous sound tracks and create marvelous sounds using music synthesizers, music originally conceived as a recording may be unplayable in live performance. These cases testify to the power of the recording art of music.

As much as we love renting movies and watching them at home on our VCR's, audiences must face the reality that home viewing of videos is not the same experience as seeing the film in a theatre. The impact of the film is always diminished on video tape. First, directors conceive their films as being shown on a large screen. The reduction of a film so that it can be seen on a 19" TV screen affects both the audience's reception of the cognitive, emotional, and aesthetic values of the film. Long shots of crowds so awe-inspiring on film become irritatingly small on the TV screen. Also, to put the film on video tape sometimes demands eliminating the action from the sides of the film frames in order to accommodate the needs of video tape. The music and sound score, amplified by stereo speakers which surround the audience in the theatre, gets reduced to coming out of one speaker or stereo speakers in the TV set; its impact is severely diminished. And, finally, the home viewing environment is the one for watching television, which interferes with the audience's abilities to empathize fully.

So, if you have ever wondered why the movie that your friends told you was wonderful was only so-so when you saw it on your VCR, you have some understanding what may have interfered with your reception of it. Some of these distractions can be controlled; for example, you could adjust environmental factors to more closely approximate those of a film theatre. However, when we watch a video tape of feature film, we must always realize that we are receiving the stimuli of a *recording art* and not the stimuli of the original film.

Video tapes of theatre and dance performances originally conceived for live performance in a theatre and not adapted for taping are notoriously unsatisfying. Even when these performances are taped before a live audience they are less satisfying than film or television drama or dance. Why?

The recording art of video tape has its own aesthetic requirements, very similar to the aesthetic of television performance. Any theatre or dance presentation must be adapted for the aesthetic requirements of video. Theatre and dance are originally produced to communicate to an audience in a theatre, and not to a camera which records the performance for an audience. Theatre and dance work best as a recorded art when they are reconceived for the camera.

Conclusion

The recording arts offer us as audiences a rich storehouse of performing arts' experiences. Because of the relatively inexpensive cost of renting a video or purchasing a music recording, the performance arts are now available to vast new audiences. The explosion in the recording arts will continue, and no doubt technology will continue to improve its ability to bring them to us with greater fidelity and quality.

The only danger the recording arts present to audiences is that they will become our exclusive choice for performing arts entertainment. The recording arts have their limits for us as audience members. They can never hope to capture the immediacy and engagement of live performances. The answer seems simple: balance your performing arts choices between the live performing arts and the recording arts. In this way you get the best of both worlds!

PART III

Criticism and the Performing Arts

Criticism is a "bad" word in our society. No one likes to be criticized. Even when we cognitively know that criticism is necessary for our growth and development, we would prefer not to hear it. Praise is always welcome. However, we do not associate "praise" with the word "criticism." Criticism suggests a negative, destructive act.

The idea of functioning as a "critic" is uncomfortable for many of us. To be such a bearer of bad tidings would mean being alienated from the majority of society. Is not the critic "more knowledgeable" and "better" than every one else? Most people truly dislike this "know-it-all," who always seems free to spout off his/her opinions. Who would want to be a critic?

These ideas about criticism and critics represent our feelings more than the reality of the situation. We daily function as "critics" in life, giving our opinions about everything from how people should live their lives to what is the best restaurant in town. When we give these opinions, we do not see ourselves as critics, but "helpers" or "insight-givers" or "experts." We feel free to speak on these issues because we have first hand knowledge and experience; we perceive that our "ideas" on these subjects have value and worth. However, even though we function as critics and dispense criticism, we choose to describe our actions using terms that are less negative: "just one man's opinion," "from the woman's point of view," "having been through the same thing myself," "I'm a mother, and I know . . .", or "not that set myself up as an expert, but . . ."

When we tell someone that we like her clothes, or his car, or when we congratulate someone for her achievement in sports or his completion of a college degree, we never perceive that we are offering criticism. However, praise may be the result of a critical act. Criticism is not just negative.

Criticism is the process of evaluating or making judgments. To do this we bring our analytical powers to bear on a situation, a person, an event, or an object. Using analysis and our knowledge and experience of the situation, person, event, or object, we form judgments—good or bad—that we share with other people. As you can see, we all daily practice the lively art of criticism.

Criticism and the Performing Arts

We treat the performing arts no differently than any other area of our lives. We share our opinions about movies, TV, musical groups, records, CD's and videos almost without being asked. We do not perceive our opinions as ''criticism,'' but of course they are.

In fact, each of us is a powerful critic. You can probably think of situations where you have influenced people to go to a movie or concert because you strongly advocated its excellence. Or, you may remember when a family member's or best friend's ''opinion'' caused you to choose a particular movie or TV show or recording. In the performing arts business your criticism is recognized as a powerful force: ''word-of-mouth.'' Every performance wants good ''word-of-mouth.'' It is the one means of promotion and publicity over which people in the business have no control. ''Word-of-mouth'' is your criticism in action.

The reality of performance insists on the critical act. You experience a play, a ballet, a symphony orchestra, a film, a TV program, radio drama, a video, or a CD. As the Performing Arts Communication Model suggests, you will have a reaction to the stimuli of the performance. These reactions will be expressed to others. These reactions will function as criticism.

The information in this book and the experience of the performances which you have been attending join to make your reactions more informed. Like everything else in life, our opinions will be listened to with greater respect if they appear based on knowledge and experience. Knowledge and experience lead to informed criticism, criticism which reveals a thoughtful evaluator. Criticism is the final part of your response to the performing arts. It cannot be avoided. It will only improve with greater knowledge and experience.

Most of all criticism is fun. Your left-hemisphere, which we have restrained throughout the present moments of receiving the stimuli of performances, now gets fully involved. In a real sense the left brain gets to ''come out and play.''

Approach the critical act ''playfully.'' This does not imply silliness or frivolity, but suggests the quality of ''play'' : committed and focused actions that bring to bear all of the mind's potentials for creativity and imagination. Analysis and evaluation does not exclude the joy and fun of creativity. The lively pleasure of two people sharing their responses to a dance concert or a film engages their verbal minds, sharpens their wits, and stimulates each to their highest powers of analytical creativity. This final part of experiencing the performing arts, in which the left brain leads, should be a whole brain experience. With the left

144

brain directing the analysis and the right brain "playing" along, the critical act becomes a truly creative one.

Taste vs. Criticism

How do we, as critics of the performing arts, avoid having our personal tastes control our responses? Part of the answer lies in understanding the differences between personal taste and criticism. They are not the same.

The often-quoted Latin maxim addresses the subject of personal taste: *De gustibus non est disputandum* (" In matters of taste there is no argument") . Tastes are simply our likes and dislikes. It is quite useless to argue about likes and dislikes because they defy the processes of reasoning. If you like green and I like blue, our personal tastes in color differ. To argue that one is better than the other is silly; no one would be able to convince the other.

De gustibus does not imply that there can not be standards of tastes. "I like ..." is merely a statement of personal taste, and not analytical judgement. Criticism of the performing arts must go beyond purely subjective comments (those comments determined only by emotional response). We must get beyond thinking that one person's opinions about the arts are as good as another's.

In many areas of our lives, we accept the idea that one person's opinions carry more weight than another's. We value the opinion of our family physician in matters of health over the insights of our best friend. We respond to the opinion of the auto mechanic in matters concerning our car over the ideas of the clerk at the dry cleaners. Quite obviously we respect the *informed* opinion, the one based on knowledge and experience.

Likewise, in evaluating the arts the informed response carries more weight. Audience members who can respond to a performance in detail and reveal their awarenesses of the significance of these details command more respect than the individuals who cannot get beyond their subjective feelings (" I liked it.") .

The informed and experienced audience member knows that there are no absolutes in the performing arts: any given performance will have its advocates and its detractors. Therefore, when we forcefully articulate our opinions of what we see and hear, we are not trying to impose our viewpoint on others. Good criticism of the arts will encourage an exchange of opinions and a free flow of ideas about the performance. Good criticism provokes delightful conversation between people, each having the right to think for himself/herself.

If your criticism is lapsing into a meaningless reiteration of personal likes or dislikes, which have little to do with a response to the performance, a failsafe method can check that your criticism is on-track. The music critic for *High Fidelity* magazine defined years ago the focus of performance evaluation:

145

In the craft of reviewing, what must be done is to state a judgment and indicate (usually in highly compressed form) the chain of argument that supports it. If the critic is doing his job properly, he will always give reasons for the conclusions he draws. These reasons will be unrelated to his personal state of mind and emotions at the moment; they will be focused on the external thing—the work of art itself.

(High Fidelity, March 1963, p.41)

Focus your responses on the work of art itself and your criticism will have aesthetic purpose and critical direction.

Critical Perspectives for Evaluating the Performing Arts

After a performance we sometimes think: "What am I going to say about it?" We may realize that repeating "I like it" is not satisfactory except as an elementary expression of personal taste. Yet the insecurity remains. Where do I begin in responding to a performance? What do I say?

Maybe the first step is to avoid using the word "criticism". Often just the idea that you must "criticize" creates a mental block to responding to a performance. Having reactions to a film, play, dance, or concert is very natural; it is impossible to sit for two hours receiving an experience as sensually stimulating as a performing art without having a reaction. So, instead of worrying about criticizing the event, just react to it.

Begin with what you liked about the performance. No matter what your overall reaction to a performance is, you will have liked something about the experience. As you start to express your "likes," you should notice that they fit in distinct categories, i.e., critical perspectives.

If your initial responses deal with the actors, musicians, dancers, camera shots, special effects, or design elements, you are using the *aesthetic* critical perspective. You are reacting to artistic elements of the performing arts. Your knowledge of and experience with the performing arts will make your comments about the aesthetic elements richer. If you concentrated during the present moments of the experience, these aesthetic responses will be more detailed and specific. As you experience more of the performing arts, you will find that you naturally begin to make contrasts and comparisons with other performances, and/or with other work by the specific artists. The aesthetic critical perspective probably comes to mind first after a performance ends.

If your initial responses deal with how the performance relates to issues in society (e.g., the elderly, war, abortion, child abuse) or universal ideas (meaning of death; love; search for self), you are using the *societal* critical perspective. Performing arts do not exist in isolation from society. Dancers, musicians, theatre artists, and filmmakers often make statements about the condition of society and of humankind through their arts. If you find yourself responding to the issues and ideas of a performance as they relate to society, you have received the artist's message. Often the arts encourage stimulating discussions of these social issues.

If your initial responses deal with how the performance relates to your own life, you are using the *individual* critical perspective. The performing arts can make us think and feel more deeply about the personal issues of our lives: relationships, family, career. Relating the performance to your life often encourages a healthy self analysis, which may lead to growth and development.

If your initial responses deal with how much pleasure the performance gave you, you are using the *entertainment* critical perspective. To entertain is to hold the attention of an audience. Entertainment does not necessarily imply "fun" ; our attention can be held by serious plays, music, and dance. However, responding with the entertainment critical perspective usually means that you were engaged by the pleasure and escape provided by the performance.

In responding to a performance the various critical perspectives often overlap. For example, a film concerned with the issue of adult children and their aging parents could be responded to as a film addressing the important social issues of nursing homes and elderly care; or as a film which encourages you to think about your elderly grandparents and the inevitable aging of your parents; or as an film well-acted and directed. All of these perspectives are valid responses to the film.

After talking about what you liked about a performance, you then can explore the problems with the event. Again, your concerns will cluster around one of the critical perspectives. As with the praise, the negative comments should use specific details and show your understanding of the performing art and its elements.

Practicing criticism gives you greater confidence. Usually we are not faced with the need to write our criticism. After viewing a performance, practice criticism in your conversations with friends. You will have the opportunity to express your views, and to listen to others' opinions. The variety of reactions to the event at first may amaze you. However, you may find yourself gaining insights into the performance because of someone else's response. Good criticism allows for the growth and development of the critic's perceptions, as well as providing the opportunity to put the critic's thoughts into words.

Good oral performance criticism demands that the responders enjoy the experience of exchanging ideas. If you should discover that your friend does not want to talk about the play/film/dance/concert, or is unwilling to listen to your perceptions, think through your reactions solitarily. You would have a reaction if you experienced a performance alone, so practicing the solitary response is useful. Besides the arts should not be the occasion for a fight over their meaning or impact. And, if you like to talk about performances, consider seeing them with friends who enjoying sharing ideas as much as you.

Criticism Is Active

Vincent Canby, the New York *Times* film reviewer, has written about responding to movies:

Audiences are drawn into movies not by the literal reality of what they're seeing but by various devices of dramatic invention that invite emotional and/or intellectual response. At their very best, movies, which we accept in a passive way, have the effect of prompting us to think and feel in such a manner that the passive experience becomes something akin to active.

What he has written about film certainly would apply to all the performing arts. Good performances are active involving experiences. Yet we often think of "action" only in terms of physical action. However, as we grow in our understanding of the performing arts, we understand that the stimulation of thoughts and emotions prompted by a performance is an extremely active process. We become involved actively through our whole brain receiving all the stimuli of the performance.

Being mentally engaged in the performance is the first step of criticism. Although the criticism occurs after the performance, it starts with our perceptions taking in all the performance has to offer. This passive experience becomes "akin to active." The critical act brings the performance experience to an active closure. Criticism is an active creative act deriving from the audience's passive reception.

Criticism and Appreciation of the Arts

Good criticism leads to a greater awareness and appreciation of the arts. Your ability to put your responses to the performing arts into words reflects your mind's engagement with the performance and your ability to use your knowledge and experience to make judgments about the experience. The more often you perform the critical act, the more sensitive you become to the performing arts and their similarities.

Similarities Among the Performing Arts

As we have studied the various performing arts, you have probably noticed similarities among the various arts. These similarities give unity to what appears to be the disparate arts of theatre, music, dance, film, television, radio, and the recording arts.

An essential feature of all the performing arts is the use of tension and release within their structures. All the performing arts use the building of tension followed by its release as part of the performance. In theatre, the drama is constructed of scenes which build the conflict and then release it; music is constructed from units of tension and release; and dancers move from tension to release with every action of the dance. These patterns of tension/release compel us to give attention to a performance.

The performing arts use the same terms, or elements. The performing arts communicate through body and/or voice; they utilize the design elements of line, mass, and color; they explore space in unique ways; rhythm is an integral feature of their structures; and

148

they all demand from their audiences a willing suspension of disbelief and the ability to react with the performance. Finally, the immediacy of the live performance moment is essential to theatre, dance, and music.

The critical act develops a true awareness of the uniqueness of the creative act. Our awareness of performing artists and the special nature of their arts grows with our study of the arts and our experiences at performances. The more we know and the more we attend plays, concerts, ballets, and films, the more the ''art'' of the performers is recognized. It becomes impossible to watch a violinist, or a ballet dancer, or an actor and not experience a sense of awe about his/her skills.

As we develop an appreciation for the performing arts, we become more aware of the requirements for the intelligent, engaged audience member. Beyond the techniques mentioned in this book, the critical act also creates criteria for ''self-censorship'' of the performing arts. Self-censorship is the only rational kind of censorship. Our knowledge and experience encourage us to attend certain performances and to avoid others. Our critical judgement sets our own censorship criteria, thereby avoiding the need of outside interference in our decision making about the performing arts. As your appreciation grows a set of criteria emerges which finds some performances acceptable and other performances wanting.

Conclusion

As audiences we must face our responsibilities at performances as much as artists who have spent years of training in order to perform. The responsibilities include preparation for and practice in responding to the performing arts. The more knowledge and experience of the performing arts that we accumulate, the more aesthetically, emotionally, and cognitively responsive our criticism will be. True appreciation may then follow. As we experience the creativity of performing artists, our lives will be richer.

Selected Bibliography

Atchity, Kenneth, *A Writer's Time*. New York: W. W. Norton, 1986.

Benedetti, Robert L., *The Actor at Work*. 3rd Ed. Englewood Cliffs, N.J.: Prentice-Hall, 1981.

Blakeslee, Thomas R., *The Right Brain*. Garden City, N.Y.: Anchor Press, 1980.

Bobker, Lee R., *Elements of Film*. New York: Harcourt, Brace, and World, Inc., 1969.

Brockett, Oscar, *The Theatre* (2nd edition). New York: Holt, Rinehart, and Winston, 1969.

Chester, G., G. R. Garrison, and E. E. Willis, *Television and Radio*. Englewood Cliffs, N.H.: Prentice-Hall, 1978.

Cohen, Robert, *Theatre*. 2nd Ed. Palo Alto, CA: Mayfield Publishing Co., 1988.

Copland, Aaron, *What to Listen for in Music*. New York: McGraw-Hill Book Co., 1939.

Corson, Richard, *Stage Makeup*. 5th Ed. New York: Appleton-Century-Crofts, 1975.

Delgado, Ramon, *Acting With Both Sides of Your Brain*. New York: Holt, Rinehart, and Winston, 1986.

Edmonds, Robert, *The Sights and Sounds of Cinema and Television*. New York: Teachers College Press, 1982.

Edwards, Betty, *Drawing on the Right Side of the Brain*. Los Angeles: J.P. Tarcher, 1979.

_____ *Drawing on the Artist Within*. New York: Simon and Schuster, 1986.

Fell, John L., *Film: An Introduction*. New York: Praeger Publishers, 1975.

Gessner, Robert, *The Moving Image: A Guide to Cinematic Literacy*. New York: E.P. Dutton, 1970.

Giannetti, Louis G., *Understanding Movies*. Englewood Cliffs, N.J.: Prentice-Hall, 1972.

Green, Barry (with W. Timothy Gallwey), *The Inner Game of Music*. New York: Anchor Press/Doubleday, 1986.

Hagen, Uta, *Respect for Acting*. New York: Macmillan, 1973.

Hanna, Judith Lynne, *The Performer-Audience Connection*. Austin, TX: University of Texas Press, 1983.

Harrington, John, *The Rhetoric of Film*. New York: Holt, Rinehart, and Winston, 1973.

Harris, Jay (editor), *TV Guide: The First 25 Years*. New York: Simon and Schuster, 1978.

Hatlen, Theodore, W., *Orientation to the Theatre*. Englewood Cliffs, N.J.: Prentice-Hall, 1987.

Hoffer, Charles R., *A Concise Introduction to Music Listening*. Belmont, CA: Wadsworth Publishing, 1974.

Hodge, Francis, *Play Directing: Analysis, Communication, and Style*. Englewood Cliffs, N.H.: Prentice-Hall, 1971.

Jones, Robert Edmund, *The Dramatic Imagination*. New York: Meredith Publishing Co., 1941.

Jowett, Garth, *Film, The Democratic Art*. Boston: Little, Brown, and Co., 1976.

Jowett, Garth, and James M. Linton, *Movies as Mass Communication.* Beverly Hills: Sage Publications, 1980.

Kamien, Roger, *Music, An Appreciation.* New York: McGraw-Hill Book Co., 1976.

Kaufman, Helen L., *The Joy in Listening.* New York: Grosset-Dunlap, 1948.

Kline, Nancy M., *Enjoying the Arts/Dance.* New York: Richard Rosens Press, 1975.

Kosslyn, Stephen Michael, *Ghosts in the Mind's Machines: Creating and Using Images in the Brain.* New York: W. W. Norton, 1983.

Machlis, Joseph, *The Enjoyment of Music.* New York: W. W. Norton, 1977.

Martin, John, *Introduction to the Dance.* Brooklyn: Dance Horizons, 1965.

McGaw, Charles J., *Acting Is Believing.* 4th Ed. New York: Holt, Rinehart, and Winston, 1980.

Mielziner, Jo, *Designing for the Theatre.* New York: Atheneum, 1965.

Miller, William Hugh, *Everybody's Guide to Music.* New York: Chilton Company, 1961.

Monaco, James, *How to Read a Film.* New York: Oxford University Press, 1981.

Nadel, Myron Howard, and Constance Nadel Miller (editors), *The Dance Experience.* New York: Universe Books, 1978.

Pilbrow, Richard, *Stage Lighting.* New York: DBS Publications, 1979.

Randolph, David, *This Is Music.* New York: Mentor Books, 1964.

Redmond, Mark, "A Multi-Dimensional Theory and Measure of Decentering." Paper presented at the annual meeting of the Speech Communication Association, Boston, MA 1987.

Redmond, Mark, "An Inclusive Conceptualization of Empathy." Paper presented at annual meeting of Speech Communication Association, Chicago, IL 1986.

Restak, Richard M., *The Brain.* New York: Bantam Books, 1984.

_____ *The Mind.* New York: Bantam Books, 1988.

Russell, Douglas, *Stage Costume Design.* New York: Appleton-Century-Crofts, 1973.

Shanks, Bob, *The Cool Fire.* New York: W. W. Norton, 1976.

Sporre, Dennis J., *Perceiving the Arts.* Englewood Cliffs, N.J.: Prentice-Hall, 1985.

Springer, Sally P., and George Deutsch, *Left Brain, Right Brain.* San Francisco: W.H. Freeman, 1981.

Styan, J. L., *The Elements of Drama.* New York: Cambridge University Press, 1960.

_____ *Drama, stage, and Audience.* New York: Cambridge University Press, 1975.

Terry, Walter, *How to Look at Dance.* New York: William Morrow, 1982.

Watts, Harris, *On Camera.* London: British Broadcasting Corporation, 1982.

Wonder, Jacquelyn, and Priscilla Donovan, *Whole Brain Thinking.* New York: Ballantine Books, 1985.

Zdenek, Marilee, *The Right Brain Experience: An Intimate Program to Free the Powers of Your Imagination.* New York: McGraw-Hill, 1983.

Glossary

acting. Conscious creative activity in which a performer using his/her voice, body, and emotion/mind simulates the behavior of a fictitious character.

aesthetic distance. The mental/physical separation or detachment from an aesthetic experience.

aesthetics. A branch of philosophy dealing with art, its creative sources, its forms, and its effects.

aftermath. What happens after a performance. An audience member's individual and group response to a performance.

art. The making or doing of things that display form, beauty, and unusual perception. The controlled structuring of a medium or a material to communicate as vividly and movingly as possible the artist's personal vision of experience. A form of knowledge which provides perceptions and insights about ourselves and the world.

audience. A group of people assembled to experience a performance.

ballet. A dance form distinguished by its emphasis on elegance, verticality, line, defiance of gravity, symmetrical movement, and the curved arm and hands. Developed in the 17th century courts of France.

blocking. A plan for controlling audience focus created by the director and using composition, movement, and actor gesture.

characters. The means the playwright must use to reveal the dramatic action, or plot of a drama.

climax. The point of highest interest in the plot of a drama.

complications. Additions to the plot which increase the tension of the conflict, and build to the climax of the play.

conflict. The strongly opposing forces within the dramatic action.

corpus collasum. A structure in the brain which connects the two hemispheres and allows for interaction between the two.

criticism. The process of evaluating and making judgments. Bringing our analytical powers to bear on a situation, a person, an event, or an object. In the performing arts criticism demands knowledge and experience of the arts, plus a sensitivity to and concentration on the performance in the present moment.

curtain call. Applause for the performers after a performance, which integrates the social and aesthetic experiences.

dance. The performing art in which the body expresses emotions and ideas through movement. It utilizes the elements of time, space, and energy, and exists in a variety of forms. Music is often the stimulus for theatrical dance.

demography. The study of characteristics of human populations. In television research organizations like the A. C. Neilsen Co. provides demographic data—e.g., size and characteristics of audiences—about programming to networks.

denouement. The last portion of the plot, which provides the unraveling, solution, or clarification, and brings to the plot to its final resolution.

design. The visual/aural scheme of the production, including scenery, costumes, properties, lighting, music/sound, and makeup.

diction. The choice of words the playwright uses to carry the dramatic action of the plot, to evolve characters, and to reveal the theme.

directing. The process of providing a unified interpretation of the play utilizing the arts of acting and design. For the audience directing provides the production concept and audience focus.

drama. A literary art written with the expressed purpose of being performed by actors before an audience. The elements of drama include: plot, characters, theme, diction, music, and spectacle.

empathy. The ability to share another's emotions or feelings, or the projection of your personality into the personality of another person or into an object in order to understand them better; with empathy you attribute to the other person or object your own emotions and responses.

energy. In dance the amount of force a dancer uses to move and/or gesture.

ephemeral. Short-lived and temporary; existing in time, e.g., a play presented in the theatre.

exposition. The beginning phase of the plot introduces the characters, the dramatic action, and the environment of the play.

feedback. Reactions to what you have heard. The reactions may be verbal, visual, or aural.

film. A uniquely visual performing art which exists for audiences as a series of images supported by dialogue, music, sound effects, and special effects.

form. The organizational structure imposed upon melody, rhythm, harmony, and tone color.

grazing. The process of watching several television programs at one time, of moving through the channels, of pausing for short intervals with certain programs, and of moving on as the program becomes less interesting.

harmony. Simultaneous sounding of two or more notes, especially when they are pleasing to the ear.

imagination. The mind's capacity to form ideal or fictional images of things that are not actually present to the senses.

immediacy. The interaction, or feedback, between the performance—either live or recorded—and the audience, which is experiencing it in the same moment.

jazz dance. A dance form distinguished by its high energy and excitement, its great flexibility in using parts of the body, its reliance on a strong underlying rhythm, and its use of isolation and syncopation of body parts.

left hemisphere. The half of the brain responsible for verbal, analytical, logical thinking.

listening. A complex behavior involving receiving and responding to aural and visual stimuli.

154

literary/visual arts. Arts created by "making" things. Arts that are fixed-in-time, meant to be responded to solitarily, and crated before the audience experiences them. Examples include the novel, poetry, sculpture, and painting.

melody. The sequence of single tones which produce a whole. The whole is the tune.

mimesis. The imitation of action.

modern dance. A 20th century dance form distinguished by its use of gravity, of swinging and pushing in/pushing out movements, of contraction, and of asymmetrical movement.

music. The performing art composed of melody, rhythm, tone color, harmony, and form. Its appeal is primarily to the right hemisphere of the brain.

performing arts. Arts created by "doing" things. Arts that are ephemeral, meant to be responded to in a group, and created at the same time the audience experiences them. Examples include live theatre, dance, and music.

plot. The story of the play, or simply what happens in the drama.

popular entertainment. An amusement or diversion for a mass audience, which uses currently dominant attitudes and interests, and integrates them with stereotyped characters, stock situations, and universally acceptable ideas.

presentational theatre. Non-illusory theatre. Actors do not lose their identities as actors. The stage is a platform for acting not a disguised area. Actors, audience, and performance exist within the same psychologically undifferentiated world.

production concept. What the director wants the audience to get from a production; what the audience should walk away with in their thoughts and feelings. The production concept unifies all the theatrical elements in a production.

radio. The conversion of sounds into electromagnetic waves which are transmitted directly through space over a distance. A major medium for the performing arts from 1929–1954 (The Golden Age of Radio).

reacting to. A reactive process of evaluating experience from your own perspective.

reacting with. A proactive process of understanding experience from another person's viewpoint, or from the aesthetic perspective.

recording arts. Arts created by "doing" things. Arts that are fixed-in-time, meant to be responded to in a group, and crated before the audience experiences them. Examples include film; musical recordings, tapes, and compact discs; and video and audio tape.

representational theatre. Illusory theatre. Theatre artists make an effort to convince the audience that a stage is not a stage, and that actors are not really actors. The stage is an area of illusion; the audience the place of actuality.

rhythm. The "beat" of music. The physical aspect of music.

right hemisphere. The half of the brain responsible for intuitive, emotional, spatial, and holistic thinking.

roleplaying or role presentation. A unified pattern of behavior revealing part of an individual's total nature.

social contagion theory. People in groups tend to react in the same ways; behavior in groups is contagious among the people in the groups.

space. The dance element which defines the dance form. How dancers use space will communicate ideas and emotions.

spectacle. All the visual elements of theatre.

stereotype. An over simplified or conventional pattern of behavior considered typical for a group, e.g., ''absent-minded professors.''

taste. In the performing arts, our likes and dislikes. A purely subjective opinion about a performing art.

technique. Acting skills that can be repeated on demand.

television. The process of transmitting sounds and images through space and over distance. The most pervasive performing art in the United States. Primarily functions as popular entertainment.

theatre. A live performance of a drama by actors before an audience.

theme. The major idea or the message of the drama.

time. An element of dance which exists primarily in rhythms and tempos.

tone color. The quality of the sound of music that encourages specific feelings toward the melody.

willing suspension of disbelief. An act of individual will power to accept the aesthetic experience in place of the ''real world'' and its social reality.

Index

159

PERFORMANCE REACTION CARD

NAME: _____

NAME OF EVENT: _____ PERFORMANCE DATE: _____

Respond in *specific detail* to the performance: 1) what really pleased you? 2) what did not "work for you?" 3) which (if any) performers were especially effective/exciting and why? 4) what was your overall reaction to the event?

PERFORMANCE REACTION CARD

NAME: _____

NAME OF EVENT: _____ PERFORMANCE DATE: _____

Respond in *specific detail* to the performance: 1) what really pleased you? 2) what did not "work for you?" 3) which (if any) performers were especially effective/exciting and why? 4) what was your overall reaction to the event?

PERFORMANCE REACTION CARD

NAME: _____

NAME OF EVENT: _____ PERFORMANCE DATE: _____

Respond in *specific detail* to the performance: 1) what really pleased you? 2) what did not
"work for you?" 3) which (if any) performers were especially effective/exciting and why?
4) what was your overall reaction to the event?

PERFORMANCE REACTION CARD

NAME: _____

NAME OF EVENT: _____ PERFORMANCE DATE: _____

Respond in *specific detail* to the performance: 1) what really pleased you? 2) what did not "work for you?" 3) which (if any) performers were especially effective/exciting and why? 4) what was your overall reaction to the event?

PERFORMANCE REACTION CARD

NAME: _____

NAME OF EVENT: _____ PERFORMANCE DATE: _____

Respond in *specific detail* to the performance: 1) what really pleased you? 2) what did not "work for you?" 3) which (if any) performers were especially effective/exciting and why? 4) what was your overall reaction to the event?

PERFORMANCE REACTION CARD

NAME: _____

NAME OF EVENT: _____ PERFORMANCE DATE: _____

Respond in *specific detail* to the performance: 1) what really pleased you? 2) what did not "work for you?" 3) which (if any) performers were especially effective/exciting and why? 4) what was your overall reaction to the event?

PERFORMANCE REACTION CARD

NAME: _____

NAME OF EVENT: _____ PERFORMANCE DATE: _____

Respond in *specific detail* to the performance: 1) what really pleased you? 2) what did not "work for you?" 3) which (if any) performers were especially effective/exciting and why? 4) what was your overall reaction to the event?

PERFORMANCE REACTION CARD

NAME: _____

NAME OF EVENT: _____ PERFORMANCE DATE: _____

Respond in *specific detail* to the performance: 1) what really pleased you? 2) what did not "work for you?" 3) which (if any) performers were especially effective/exciting and why? 4) what was your overall reaction to the event?

PERFORMANCE REACTION CARD

NAME: _____

NAME OF EVENT: _____ PERFORMANCE DATE: _____

Respond in *specific detail* to the performance: 1) what really pleased you? 2) what did not "work for you?" 3) which (if any) performers were especially effective/exciting and why? 4) what was your overall reaction to the event?

PERFORMANCE REACTION CARD

NAME: _____

NAME OF EVENT: _____ PERFORMANCE DATE: _____

Respond in *specific detail* to the performance: 1) what really pleased you? 2) what did not "work for you?" 3) which (if any) performers were especially effective/exciting and why? 4) what was your overall reaction to the event?